Your Towns and Cities in th

Bognor in the Great War

Your Towns and Cities in the Great War

Bognor in the Great War

Cliff Mewett

Pen & Sword
MILITARY

First published in Great Britain in 2014 by
PEN & SWORD MILITARY
an imprint of
Pen and Sword Books Ltd
47 Church Street
Barnsley
South Yorkshire S70 2AS

ISBN 978 1 78346 282 7

A CIP record for this book is available from the British Library

Printed and bound in England
by CPI Group (UK) Ltd, Croydon, CR0 4YY

Typeset in Times New Roman by Chic Graphics

Pen & Sword Books Ltd incorporates the imprints of
Pen & Sword Archaeology, Atlas, Aviation, Battleground, Discovery,
Family History, History, Maritime, Military, Naval, Politics, Railways,
Select, Social History, Transport, True Crime, and Claymore Press,
Frontline Books, Leo Cooper, Praetorian Press, Remember When,
Seaforth Publishing and Wharncliffe.

For a complete list of Pen and Sword titles please contact
Pen and Sword Books Limited
47 Church Street, Barnsley, South Yorkshire, S70 2AS, England
E-mail: enquiries@pen-and-sword.co.uk
Website: www.pen-and-sword.co.uk

Contents

Acknowledgements

My grateful thanks to the staff at the West Sussex Records Office, Chichester, for their help in researching this book. The majority of the book is taken from the local newspapers of the time, the *Bognor Observer* and the West Sussex Gazette, which are held in their archives. The photographs unless specifically acknowledged, are from the Bognor Regis Local History Society.

Introduction

An assassin's bullet in far off Sarajevo on 28 June 1914 seemed a world away from Bognor, an assassination that would over the next four years affect almost every family in the town. As a result of the assassination of Archduke Franz Ferdinand, Austria-Hungary declared war on Serbia, Russia mobilized to assist Serbia and Germany then declared war on Russia, who in turn had a pact with France. Britain, somewhat on the sidelines, had a treaty obligation to protect Belgium's neutrality and, as the August Bank Holiday weekend approached the international crises gathered pace.

On Saturday 1 August Germany invaded Luxemburg; France and Belgium mobilized and the British called up their Naval Reservists. The following day, Bank Holiday Sunday, 2 August, the British daily papers made an unusual Sunday appearance, selling out in hours. In London, crowds of several thousands marched to Buckingham Palace, singing the British and French national anthems, cheering wildly as King George V and Queen Mary came out on to the balcony to receive them. War fever was spreading. In Europe, Germany issued an ultimatum to Belgium 'requesting' permission to march troops through that country, making it clear that dire circumstances would follow a refusal. On Bank Holiday Monday, 3 August, as Parliament met, Germany declared war on France and Belgium refused to allow German troops through her territory, appealing to King George for assistance. In response, the British Government demanded assurances from Germany that Belgium's neutrality would be respected, it also announced that British naval mobilization had been completed. Throughout Tuesday 4 August, Britain awaited the German reply to the ultimatum, which was due by eleven o'clock that evening. No reply was forthcoming and as eleven o'clock struck a message was sent to the Royal Navy, 'Commence hostilities against Germany'. The Great War had begun.

Cliff Mewett

CHAPTER 1

Bognor Mobilizes

Pre War Bognor

The summer of 1914 was following its usual pattern; the 'season' was in full swing with hotels, guest and lodging houses all full. Bognor was enjoying an excellent year; the numbers of enquiries received from prospective visitors in the early summer were 'three times the number of previous years'.

'Excursionists still continue to pour into the town and generally speaking the weather has been very propitious', reported the *Bognor Observer* in July, 'This week another ten thousand are expected. Last Monday, with several Sunday School Excursions, a "Cook" and a good many adults, the total was 1440; and yesterday's total was 2050. Today 1770 are expected. It seems to be the rule that the biggest numbers come on Wednesdays, which is unfortunate as the shops for the most part are closed. On Thursday 1100 are coming and on Friday 530. On Saturday there will be another of "Cooks" excursions with a small party of adults.'

Visitors and locals were entertained at the Olympian Gardens by Wallis Arnold's revue and the newly refurbished pier was doing well, with its attractions of a theatre, cinema and thousands taking a stroll 'out to sea'. Further along the eastern Esplanade, the Kursaal was also doing good business, offering skating, hockey matches, boxing matches and a good theatre where the George Edwardes Company was performing 'The Marriage Market'. The pony and donkey men were delighting children with rides along the sand, whilst the bathing machines were busy transporting their customers to the briny. In the afternoons and evenings the sound of the Band of the 2nd Dragoon Guards, performing alternately in both the western and eastern bandstands to appreciative audiences, filled the air. Both the Bognor Town and North Bersted Bands also had full programmes and Arthur Davies' Lady Car Char-a-Banc trips to Arundel, Chichester and Goodwood were as always popular, as were trips out to sea, courtesy of the local boatmen. Another attraction was the Curtis Flying Boat, based at nearby Middleton, which was frequently in the skies over Bognor, giving pleasure trips.

Local events included the Pagham and Aldwick Horticultural Show, which was successfully held although 'rain had spoilt the attendances', but the Felpham Flower Show a week later had a sunnier reception. Meanwhile, up at Nyewood Lane, Bognor Football Club was in training for its first season in the Senior Division of the West Sussex League.

Behind all these peacetime activities, speculation that Great Britain would be drawn into a European war was sweeping the country and, with King George V breaking with tradition by not attending Glorious Goodwood in July, 'being detained in London because of the foreign crises', war began to look a certainty.

Horses being requisitioned in Waterloo Square. 2 August 1914. (Sylvia Olliver)

The first visible war related activity in Bognor occurred on Friday 31 July, with the arrival home of soldiers from the Sussex Yeomanry, who had been spending a fortnight in camp at Lewes, and troops of the Army Veterinary Corps, who set up a base in the meadow at Waterloo Square and proceeded to stop and requisition horses.

> 'Considerable excitement was caused at Bognor on Friday morning, by the inspection of a large number of horses, which was carried out by the military, aided by the police. About fifty horses were drawn up against the south rail of the Merchant Taylors enclosure in Waterloo Square, while several drivers of vehicles along the front had their vans boarded by soldiers. A large crowd had assembled and by midday quite a number of vehicles were standing about in the vicinity of the pier, minus their means of locomotion.'

The scenes at Waterloo Square that day must have been heartbreaking as the horses were taken from their owners, who received a small receipt for them from the military. Many millions of horses were to serve on all sides during the conflict with a large number of them being killed, whilst others that were injured were successfully returned to duty after treatment in the Veterinary Hospitals. It is almost certain that none of the horses recruited in Bognor that day ever came back. After examination by the Army Veterinary Corps, the horses were taken by the Sussex Yeomanry to Bognor Railway Station and transported to Canterbury.

Horses were requisitioned throughout Sussex; four local National Reservists returned to Bognor that day after a successful trip:

> 'Four of the oldest members of the Bognor Division of the National Reserve have been engaged in the past week in requisitioning horses for war. Private Skinner, Private James, Private Spillatt and Sergeant Major May, who fought at Ladysmith, returned to Bognor on Sunday, having secured thirty six horses from Brighton and ten from Chichester and during the whole time did not take their boots off. They are now awaiting further orders.'

Sad scenes as owners bid farewell to their horses. Within hours they were entrained to Canterbury for war duties. (Sylvia Olliver)

(*Sergeant May was a remarkable soldier, a long serving veteran, who had fought at the Siege of Ladysmith in 1900. Now retired, he spent the years leading up to the Great War living in West Street, Bognor, from where he formed the Bognor Boys. This was a semi military youth club, which, as well as citizenship training, formed a marching band, took part in parades and provided recruits for the Army. He was particularly active within Bognor during the early days of the Great War and is consequently mentioned quite regularly in this book*).

As the likelihood of war grew, the Government called up the country's reservists, of whom there were many living in Bognor:

The Royal Navy Reserves

By what can be described as a remarkable stroke of good fortune, in March 1914 the Admiralty decided to place every ship in home waters on a war footing during the summer as an exercise scheduled to run for eleven days from 15 July. Subsequently the Naval Mobilisation Flag was hoisted at the Portsmouth Naval Base, and some 30,000 men, the whole of the Royal Fleet Reserve, were called up. Well over a hundred men from the Bognor district were serving in the Royal Navy, the Royal Naval Reserve and the Royal Marines and they 'flocked into the Naval Barracks'. In a very short time all the ships were fully manned and ready for sea. Thus the Royal Navy was ahead of the game and on 29 July, in the face of an ever worsening situation, a force of some 180 battleships, cruisers and destroyers 'steamed out from their various ports to take up positions in readiness for war'.

It soon became apparent that the numbers of men reporting for duty in the Navy far exceeded the Admiralty's requirements for the manning of ships. Accordingly, those who were surplus to the Navy's requirements were organized into Army type units, initially under Admiralty command. The scheme was the brainchild of Winston Churchill, the then First Lord of the Admiralty and earned the nickname 'Winston's Little Army'. Several Bognor men were to serve in the Royal Naval Division.

The Army Reservists

Regular soldiers signed on for seven years, after which they were committed to a further five years in the Regular Army Reserve, effectively returning to civilian life, but subject to an instant recall in the case of war or national emergency. Some forty men formed the Bognor Division who were attending their annual camps in July, with over 3000 troops of 1st Infantry Brigade billeted at nearby Goodwood, consisting of a battalion each of the Coldstream Guards, the Royal Munster Fusiliers, the Black Watch and the Scots Guards, as well as units from the Royal Field Artillery and the Hussars. In the days preceding the Declaration of War, many Bognorians travelled to Goodwood to visit the troops training and listen to their evening band concerts. Their camp was bought to an abrupt halt when the Brigade was marched to Midhurst, whence the men were taken to Aldershot by train to await further orders.

The 9th Hampshire (Cyclist) Battalion had also been based locally under canvas between Bognor and Chichester; and were also recalled:

> 'At midnight on Friday the 9th Hampshire (Cyclist) Battalion received a hasty call. During the week they had been at work between Chichester and Bognor and on Friday evening they were called away and the military authorities commenced the work of appropriating all available motor traffic. In the course

The Commer Cars of Arthur Davies at Goodwood. A few days later they were used to transport troops as war fever mounted.

> of the evening several large tourist cars from Southsea arrived and these were soon confiscated, together with other private and business cars owned by local people. A large pantechnicon arrived from Southampton and this figured in the procession, together with local brewers' vans and a contingent of Mr Davies' spacious Bognor Commer cars. Into this miscellaneous assortment of motor traffic the cyclists and their machines were hurried. Dozens of cyclists rode off on their machines and a large crowd accorded the men three hearty cheers as they went off in a westerly direction'.

Within a few weeks the 9th Hampshires returned to Bognor and set up camp on Nyewood Lane Cricket Ground in readiness for any invasion threat. With the approach of winter they were re-settled into what is now Ashley House, the Rock Buildings and Bognor Pier. They entrenched and patrolled the coast from Felpham to Selsey Bill.

The Territorial Army

The Territorial Army was formed in 1908, combining the old Volunteers, the Militia and the Yeomanry into one new force. They were all part-time volunteer soldiers, primarily for home defence. Locally, many Bognor men were in the Territorials, serving with 4th Battalion Royal Sussex Regiment. They went to their annual summer camp at Bordon, Hampshire on Sunday 26 July and were scheduled to stay there until 2 August. The Bognor Detachment consisted of some sixty soldiers, leaving by train at 10 am and picking up the Eastergate Detachment at Barnham Station. From Liphook they had a six mile march to Bordon Camp, where they joined the rest of the Home Counties Division, some 16,000 men in all. Training at Bordon began in earnest, with fitness being a key part.

Britain's Declaration of War was announced late in the evening of 4 August and the Territorials, now back from their Bordon Camp, were immediately called up. Having said their farewells, they mustered at Chichester and were transported to Newhaven. They were seen off by 'great crowds' at Chichester Railway Station, having marched from their barracks accompanied by the Regimental and Chichester City Bands.

> 'On Wednesday the Territorials complied with an order to mobilize by assembling at the Old Depot in East Row (Chichester) and at half past three they were marched to the railway station, there to entrain for Newhaven. Captain WH Kendaline was in command and Lieutenant Medlycot also accompanied the men, who marched down East Street and South Street with a fine swing and in good spirits. As they passed North Pallant they were given a farewell cheer by the people who were gathered there and they were cheered again when the train

Territorials leaving Bognor railway station for annual camp, a few days before being called up for war. (Sylvia Olliver)

The Territorials leaving for Newhaven and 'marching with a fine swing'.

> steamed out of the station just before four o'clock. They went by special train picking up the remainder of the Battalion, including contingents from Bognor, Eastergate and Arundel en route at Barnham. At every crossing and station en route people thronged to wave and cheer the train as it swept past, the soldiers responding likewise.'

As constituted, the Territorials were not obligated to operate overseas, but within weeks of the outbreak of the war they volunteered to do so, almost to a man, following the example of the Northumberland Hussars and the London Scottish Regiment.

The Special Reserve

The Special Reservists were volunteers who had spent six months in the Regular Army and then returned to their civilian lives, albeit still receiving a small Army income, which ensured their recall to the

Colours should hostilities break out. Locally they served in 3rd Battalion Royal Sussex Regiment. This Special Reserve Battalion was also attending its annual camp that July and consisted of some 350 Sussex men, including men from Bognor. Their camp was preceded by a five day march the length of the County, 'recruiting nearly fifty men whilst on the road'. Upon their arrival at Arundel they were met by the band of 4th Battalion, the Royal Sussex Regiment. After an overnight rest in Arundel, whose residents had been entertained by the band the previous evening, the march continued to Chichester 'where they were met by flag waving citizens'. They then went to their annual camp, which was interrupted on Wednesday 29 July when they received orders to go directly to Newhaven and left on the 9.30pm train, 'leaving to the rousing cheers of all the other Companies'. War fever was mounting.

The Sussex Yeomanry

The Sussex Yeomanry, in which eighty Bognor men were serving, were also attending their two week annual camp in July 1914, on the Downs south of Lewes. They were also immediately called up and sent to Canterbury, Kent.

Men of the Sussex Yeomanry mustering in Bognor prior to their annual camp in 1911.

CHAPTER 2

Recruitment

Your King and Country called you
You answered to a man
You know your country needs you
To do the best you can.

Brave hearts the trumpet calls you
The rattle of the drums
You love your mother country
And long to shame the Huns.

Your King and Country want you
To fight for right and win
Brave brothers all united
To rally round your King.

You'll keep the old flag flying
With hands across the foam
In brotherhood undying
You'll all come marching home

You'll fight boys and you'll conquer
And all the world will say
They fought those bonnie Bognor boys
Till victory crowns the day.

Field Marshal Earl Kitchener, probably Britain's best known soldier at that time, was on leave in the UK in July 1914 from his position as the Military Governor of Egypt and was due to sail back abroad on 2 August. His sailing was cancelled and the day after war broke out Prime Minister Herbert Asquith appointed him the Secretary of State

for War, with the task of 'recruiting a large army to fight Germany'. Kitchener was fully aware that Britain's regular Army, although excellent soldiers, was a woefully small force in comparison to the German hordes. He therefore immediately requested Parliamentary permission to form a New Army to serve for a period of three years, or for the duration of the war. New recruits had to fit the same criteria as the regulars regarding age and height; however, those who had previously served were accepted up to the age of 45. Public support for recruitment was initially enthusiastic, with many letters and poems urging men to enlist published in the local press.

Recruitment marches took place around Bognor, often lead by the Church Lads Brigade Band and ending at the Bedford Street Drill Hall. One such march was followed in the evening by a recruitment meeting at the Queen's Hall (now the Picturedrome) with the Red Cross Nurses, the Bognor Fire Brigade and the Town Band present. Organized by Colonel Fryer JP and Town Councillor Mr Staffurth, 'stirring speeches' were made by Recruiting Officers, after which came the call for volunteers and 'young Bognor stepped forward'; it would be all over by Christmas!

The drums of the Church Lads Brigate beat as a recruiting march parades through Bognor led 'in civvies' by Sergeant Major May.

(*Colonel Fryer was a retired officer who had served with the Suffolk Regiment. Living in Park Road, he was soon established as a leading light in the affairs of Bognor, serving as a Justice of the Peace, Town Councillor, President of the Cricket Club, the Croquet Club, etc. His name appears quite regular in this book.*)

The following day all the new recruits were marched to Bognor Station and taken to Chichester 'where they presented themselves to the Depot'. Here they were medically examined, given a New Testament to hold while they were sworn in and a pay book in which was recorded their shilling a day. After a few days they were sent to the training camps.

The Southdown Battalions

Recruiting continued apace. Lieutenant Colonel Claude Lowther MP and resident at Herstmonceux Castle, East Sussex, took the lead in forming three South Downs Battalions, which were to evolve into 11th, 12th and 13th Battalions The Royal Sussex Regiment. These were known as the Southdowners or Lowther's Lambs. The 11th Battalion

was raised on 7 September, with 'D' Company's recruitment concentrating on men from Bognor and Chichester. A recruiting map of Sussex showing the numbers of available men of the right age group was published, indicating that there were 1050 in Bognor. Very quickly the first battalion was formed; however, more men were needed and in an open letter Lieutenant Colonel Lowther wrote:

> 'Lord Kitchener has paid us the single honour of asking for a second Southdown's Battalion which together with the present Battalion will form part of his New Army. Every Englishmen must have followed with just pride the glorious achievements of our men in the field. There is no Sussex man who has not felt that his place should be by the side of those who are defending their country, their homes and their hearths, against what must prove to be insuperable odds. If every available man should come forward now and declare to the world the might of the British nation, it is up to every one of you to prove your manhood. You can best protect your homes, your wives and your children by joining the ranks. Let no man feel he is not wanted.

> I therefore call upon every man with red blood in his veins to join the Southdown Battalions of the Royal Sussex Regiment. You will not be separated, together you will train, together you will fight and together you will die if necessary. May God protect you and bring you back safely.'

The *Bognor Observer* reported:

> 'Recruiting for the Southdown Battalions of the Royal Sussex Regiment continues briskly in Bognor and District, the Recruiting Offices in York Chambers are open from 8am to 10am in the morning and 2pm to 3pm in the afternoon and from 7pm to 8pm in the evenings and on Sundays where 'a very good number are received between 10 and 11am'. Sergeant May, acting as a Recruiting Officer, receives names and is kept pretty busy at times swearing in recruits. The recruiting staff have been considerably assisted during the past two weeks by the presence of Mr Andrew Clark, a personal friend of Lt Col Lowther, who has been scouring Bognor and District beating up recruits and has had considerable success. A number of very capable and eligible men have passed through.'

Another friend of Colonel Lowther was Mr HJ Grisewood, of the Den, Bognor, who was 'enthusiastically applauded' when he appeared at a recruiting meeting on the Pier and made 'a little speech appealing for recruits'. As well as being a personal friend of Colonel Lowther, he was also Lieutenant Colonel Grisewood, although that evening he was talking as a civilian. He earnestly appealed to all the local ladies to try and get another hundred men to enlist from Bognor to serve side by side with the recruits from Chichester, Littlehampton and Arundel.

Over the following week some 238 recruits were accommodated at the Queens Hall, before leaving by train for Chichester under the watchful eye of Sergeant Major May. All the recruits for the Southdowners were sent to the camp at Cooden, near Bexhill, where over the next months they completed their training, eventually being absorbed into the army's order of battle.

Young Bognor volunteers about to 'present themselves at the depot'.

Young Southdowns recruits under the command of Colonel Fryer.

The Order of the White Feather

The 'giving' of white feathers as a show of cowardice to young men who, it was thought, should be 'wearing the khaki' emerged in 1914, with several incidents recorded in Bognor. Lieutenant Colonel Grisewood's appeal to the ladies struck a chord with one who, describing herself as 'one of the girls', wrote to the *Bognor Observer:*

> 'There are too many young men in Bognor. One meets them at every turn, tall well built fellows, lounging along the Promenade or down the High Street, with their hands in their pockets or tearing around on motor cycles, displaying a flag to show what pathetic boys they are. In times of peace these fellows are well enough, but now the place should be devoid of young men. Let Bognor be the most eager to supply gallant men to defend our well loved land. We girls should do what I think other girls of another watering place are doing, band together and give a white feather to every able bodied young man we meet. Girls of Bognor do your part! Give the cold shoulder to all the men until they don the khaki and show what stuff they are made of. The Germans need showing their places and the men of Bognor can help to do it. At present we don't think much of them.'

Replying the following week, 'one of the boys' wrote:

> 'I cannot think that it is an English girl who has written the letter to your paper last week. In the first place I entirely disagree that there are too many young men about. There are far fewer than I have seen before. Then is it not possible that those who do walk about on the Promenade are only waiting to join their Regiment, or are forced to stay behind to help in their father's business, while the older sons go out to fight? I cannot help thinking that 'one of the girls' should be better employed working for the Red Cross than distributing white feathers and I certainly think that there are many girls who would do well to put on some petticoats, before they tell the young men what to do. When these young men are in the King's uniform, they would be better employed in doing their duties, than in walking about with one of the girls.'

The indiscriminate distributing of white feathers annoyed many people, especially when they were handed mistakenly to soldiers on leave and in civilian clothes:

'Is it possible to teach certain Bognorians to behave?' wrote one angry resident. 'A Canadian soldier from the Front with his hand so wounded from a bullet passing down the centre, that his fingers were useless, was accosted in the street by a young lady who offered him a white feather. He was so incensed he said he felt like slapping her!'

Even soldiers home on leave and spending sometime in civilian clothes were mistakenly abused:

> 'Last Friday H—— C—— home from the trenches, where he had left his mate and school fellow, Frank Shrubb, felled by a shell, was riding with his young brother, who was delivering goods at Bognor. He had come straight from the trenches with vermin, mud and blood on his clothes, which he left with his mother to endeavour to clean and repair and was compelled to wear civilian clothes. Seven days leave, one spent coming, one spent in returning and five left in dear old England and this is the reception he meets.'

The Church Lads' Brigade

The Church Lads' Brigade was formed nationally in 1892, the first boys organisation to become cadets and over the years furnished a steady supply of recruits for the Army.

The Bognor and Bersted Company first paraded in 1900 and in the years preceding the outbreak of the Great War some 300 lads were trained and disciplined, a large number of whom were reported as 'doing well in the world'.

When the war commenced more youngsters were encouraged to join, as the *Bognor Observer* reported:

> 'More recruits are needed for the Bognor and Bersted Companies of the Church Lads Brigade. Members to be eligible for enlistment for this highly appreciated movement should be between 14 and 18 years of age and they should give their names to one of the Officers at the Drill Hall. A club night of boxing, fencing and games, etc., is held on Tuesdays and drill, rifle drill

and bayonet practice being carried out on Thursdays. Route marches and field days are held occasionally and a Church Parade every month. The Church Lads Brigade are regulated under War Office instructions and are supplied with khaki uniforms.'

(*Over 120 members of the Bognor Church Lads' Brigade joined the Colours. Four members were commissioned and many others became NCOs. One member was awarded the Croix de Guerre and two others the Distinguished Conduct Medal. On the downside seventeen former members were killed and three were reported missing, presumed killed.*)

CHAPTER 3

Bognor Goes to War – The Home Front

The Declaration of War saw life in Bognor change rapidly. It commenced over the August Bank Holiday weekend, the Government ordering the banks to stay closed for another three days in order to prevent a run on gold. They re-opened on Friday 7 August, the Chancellor of the Exchequer pointing out that 'the person who goes to the bank and demands all his gold is as effectively assisting the enemy as if he were to take up arms against Britain'. Treasury Notes to the value of ten shillings and one pound were issued and these with Postal Orders were now legal tender 'and cannot be refused'.

Some grocery shops that had also been closed for a couple of days, re-opening by the weekend, 'when the working classes get their wages'. In order to prevent a great rush of customers, a system of letting only three customers at a time to enter certain shops was introduced.

The Defence of the Realm Act

The Defence of the Realm Act (DORA), giving the Government wide ranging powers, was passed on 8 August 1914. This law was designed to help prevent an invasion and to keep up a high morale at home. At sometime or other during the conflict it would affect everybody. Alcohol consumption was restricted by the alteration of the licensing hours that public houses were allowed to open. These were reduced to just six hours a day, from noon till 3.00pm and 6.30pm until 9.30pm and later on they were further reduced. Customers in pubs were not allowed to buy rounds of drinks; added to this alcohol was watered down, therefore becoming less potent. Flying a kite, a favourite children's pastime, was banned for fear of attracting Zeppelins; bonfires and fireworks were banned for the same reason. The purchase of binoculars was banned, as was the feeding of bread to horses and chickens, in case of a food shortage. Military and Naval matters were not to be discussed in public places, or rumours spread about military matters. Trespassing on railway lines or bridges was banned, as was the purchase of brandy and whisky from railway refreshment rooms. The ringing of church bells was banned. The Government could censor newspapers, take over any land, factory or workshop they wanted and stop people writing abroad using invisible ink! As the war progressed so DORA was amended as required; the introduction of British Summer Time to give more daylight for extra work was one example.

The Belgium Refugees

The influx of refugees from Belgium during the autumn of 1914 provided Bognorians with their first tangible evidence that the war was raging just across the Channel. Arriving confused, frightened and carrying their worldly goods, they were soon settled in various places throughout the town, including the Princess Mary Home in Aldwick Road, which had previously been the Seaside Branch of the East London Hospital for Children, the Princess Mary Memorial Home and the Victorian Home for Women on the Eastern Esplanade, Bognor Council waving the rates for these properties to assist with their expenses. Others helped with the expenditure:

> 'One way or another little Felpham has raised about £70 and provided a number of garments towards the relief fund for the destitute Belgian refugees.'
>
> 'Belgian refugees of the upper social classes established in a temporary home expressed pleased surprise at finding Bognor such a bright and modern town. The sight of rows of smart new shops impressed them most favourably and they were surprised to learn that Bognor supported a theatre of its own.'

Opened in April 1906, the Princess Mary Memorial Home was used to house Belgian refugees in 1914.

Bognorians rallied round them and very soon a committee was established to take care of the Belgian mothers and children. They did them proud at Christmas 1914, providing the refugees with a Christmas party in the gymnasium at Northcliffe School. With well-spread tables, the little ones enjoyed a happy time with music, games, toys and many useful presents. The National Anthems were sung, La Marseillaise in French, the Brabaconne in Flemish and God Save the King in English.

M. Paul Leyder, the leader of the Belgians said 'the Friends of the Belgian's in Bognor have not only helped them bear their sorrows of exile, but have tried in every possible way to make the Belgium children forget the cruelties of war. The Belgians will never forget the kindnesses that the people of Bognor have shown them'.

Aliens

The day after war was declared the Government passed the Alien Registration Act, which required all 'foreign born residents not naturalised and still subjects or citizens of a foreign Country', to register with the police and ensure that their movements were known.

> 'However law abiding they may be it is the duty of all Aliens remaining in England to register their addresses at once and the police should be notified if it is known that any are residing in this locality, in order that their whereabouts may be officially known.'

John Armsden, of 6 The Parade, London Road, Bognor, ran a stationery shop and for no apparent reason was singled out by many people as being German, which not only affected him personally, but also his business. In order to stop the abuse he was getting he wrote to the *Bognor Observer*:

> 'Will you allow me to say that I am not German or an Alien, our name is well known enough in Bedford, the town which has known five generations of us. I and my brother are beyond the military age, but my sister has two sons fighting with the Colours and one of Mrs Armsden's brothers is a Sergeant in the Oxfordshire Yeomanry and the other is a Sergeant in the Oxford and Bucks Light Infantry. I have made this disclaimer, which is both explicit and undeniable, as the rumour was getting more persistent than pleasant for both myself and my friends.'

Hoteliers, guest and lodging housekeepers had to maintain a register of any alien residents at their establishments. Were they *bonafide* guests or were they spies? Penalties were quite severe for those who failed to follow the law. Bognor, being a busy seaside town, had many visitors and more than its fair share of aliens; most were registered with the local police and had in their possession an Identity Book. Those who were not registered found themselves in trouble.

The wife of an Austrian soldier who had moved to Bognor from London was arrested using a false name and interned. Many others were arrested as the war progressed and fined, including hotel and lodging house keepers who, ignoring the regulations, continued to take in aliens at their premises. For example, one Anna Simon, a visitor, was summoned for being an alien and entering a prohibited area without her Identity Book duly filled in. She was fined twenty shillings. Ernest James Lunn, who owned the guest house in the Steyne where

Anna was staying, was also summoned for not keeping a Register of Aliens at his lodging house. He was fined thirty shillings.

There were a good many cases of hoteliers and lodging housekeepers failing to maintain their registers which ended in prosecutions and heavy fines.

The Bognor Civil Guard

With the fear of an invasion taking place, unofficial defence volunteers, funded and organized in many cases by retired military or police officers, sprang up all over the country. Bognor was no exception, with Captain A. St. John Ingle, late of the Indian Police, who had retired to Selwood Lodge, Victoria Drive, Bognor, forming a Civil Guard of volunteers to protect Bognor from spies and infiltrators:

> 'A Civil Guard, which already includes from seventy to eighty men, has been formed in Bognor and is acting under Captain Ingle, a retired Captain of the Indian Police. It is warranted to act and is doing useful patrol duty every day and night. All males over the age of fifteen are being invited to join the Guard and the administration has been put on a very businesslike and practical footing. All members have been supplied with powerful electric lamps supplied by Captain Ingle.'

Although well organised, the Civil Guard had a short life, before being disbanded by the Home Office. Initially they sent Captain Ingle a post card informing him that definite instructions from the War Office were 'that you are not to carry firearms nor make any arrest', but to report to the police 'any suspicious person or circumstances'. Then in the last week of August orders were received to disband immediately, advising that his members, if they wished to continue to serve, should become Special Constables.

Special Constables

Among the Army Reservists and Territorials called up were several local policemen who had to be replaced and police numbers had to be increased to deal with possible unrest. The Government therefore authorized the recruitment of Special Constables and in Bognor twenty six were initially sworn in, each being issued with a truncheon, a whistle, a notebook and an armlet. Men up to the age of 50 were eligible for Special Police service. The age was to rise to seventy and their numbers to one hundred before the end of the war. Known by the number of their warrant cards, it was to be some time before they were issued with proper uniforms. The Government paid the Specials half the pay of an ordinary Police Constable, but desired that 'unpaid forces should be constituted of men desiring to serve their Country in the most useful way under the present conditions'. Two Special Constables were appointed for Aldwick, whilst Pagham had five.

An early task for the Specials was to visit every home in Bognor to ascertain what weaponry was available in the event of an invasion, a move not popular with some residents. Alfred Jones, of Tennyson Road, Bognor, expressed his views in a letter to the Editor of the *Bognor Observer*:

> 'The Police are calling at all houses in Bognor to find out what firearms are in them; I suppose it is thus expected if Germans landed here the public are to stand, with arms folded and calmly see our wives and children cruelly used and wait until a British force comes to overcome, if possible, the enemy and that would, in all probability be after my wife and child had been murdered, or worse treated. No! the subject is too serious for the public or individual. The laws of war have in every respect been ignored by Germany, and are the British public to respect these laws when dealing with the Germans, even to see their children slaughtered and never raise their hands to defend or avenge them?'

The Boy Scouts

One valuable source of 'volunteers' were the Boy Scouts, who were immediately used on a national basis, locally patrolling the Bognor to Chichester and Bognor to Littlehampton roads. They also patrolled the railway lines, the adjacent telegraph lines and checked that the railway bridges remained intact, thus ensuring there would be no disruption in communications, that could affect the mobilization of troops and the transmission of military despatches. They were also engaged by the Coastguards, where they were of 'immense service' as Coast Watchers, patrolling from Littlehampton to Selsey Bill, reporting on shipping

Bognor's Boy Scouts on parade shortly before the war's declaration.

movements and keeping a sharp lookout for 'spies and saboteurs', a task which they undertook with some enthusiasm. These patrols also took place at night, from sunset to sunrise, watching for any signs of scare attacks by the enemy.

> 'Anyone who has walked over ten miles of shingle in the dark can appreciate this is not playing at Scouting,' said the proud Scoutmaster, Mr Polhill. 'I have made a point of patrolling on the same rounds myself at night and have never failed to find our Scouts keenly on the watch.'

'Few townspeople have any idea of how useful the Scouts have been since the outbreak of war', commented the *Bognor Observer*. Boy Scouts were issued with cloth badges denoting the number of days' service they performed and would receive national recognition before the end of the war.

The Bognor Fire Brigade

The Bognor Fire Brigade went on to a war footing immediately. Air

1911 and the Bognor Fire Brigade parade on the occasion of King George V's Coronation.

raids were the threat and two firemen were kept on night duty, manning the station in case of a raid. The members of the Brigade joined the Red Cross and were paid 3s 6d a day to be taught first aid. The Sussex Yeomanry, having emptied the stables of Bognor by compulsorily commandeering the horses for military duty, caused problems for the Brigade, who struggled at times to obtain their locomotive power. Special Constables were trained by the Brigade in fire fighting to provide extra night cover and to replace those who had enlisted.

His Majesty's Coastguards

The Felpham Coastguards formed a vital link in the nation's defences. For some seventy years His Majesty's Coastguards had come under naval control and a Coastguard Station had been built in Felpham. During the war, as well as their Coastguard duties, they provided the 'firing parties', when called on to perform at local military funerals.

Felpham Coastguard Station.

The Bognor Red Cross

The Bognor Red Cross had their headquarters at Hambledon Chambers in London Road, from where they appealed for blankets, sheets, pillow cases, bolster cases, tables, medicine, trays, utensils, cloths, hot water bottles, roller towels and bandages of all description. They were also arranging local hospital emergency accommodation to cater for the expected influx of casualties. Shortly after the outbreak of war their premises were inspected and approved by the War Office for the nursing of wounded soldiers. For the inspection, 'the headquarters made a favourable impression, the rooms which were entirely transformed had the appearance of an up to date hospital. On entering, one passed through a reception room, a first aid ward, an out patients dept to the medical and surgical ward and thence to the operating theatre and kitchen. A number of boy scouts acted as patients and the nurses were drilled by Sergeant Major May.'

Built in 1895 as an asylum, the Government announced in March 1915 that it would be taking over the thousand beds at Graylingwell Hospital, Chichester for the duration of the war. The Bognor Red Cross worked very closely with the St John's Ambulance Brigade, with both

The Bognor Red Cross, c.1914.

their names being written on the sides of the two motor ambulances which operated from Bognor. These cost £250 each and were used extensively by both organisations in the ferrying of casualties from Chichester Railway Station to both the West Sussex Hospital at Chichester and the Graylingwell War Hospital.

Despite many Bognor Red Cross volunteers joining the Colours, they could still muster a credible forty two members whose workload had increased considerably with the opening of Graylingwell, with every Red Cross man having to work there as orderlies for two nights a week. Twelve Red Cross nurses from Bognor were on permanent duty at Graylingwell, carrying out two shifts a day, one from early morning till lunchtime, the other taking over until the evening, However, all Red Cross members were registered as Special Constables, which provided them with compensation if they were injured in the course of their duties, a recognition of their dedication to the war effort.

The Bognor Red Cross continued to send staff to work at Graylingwell Hospital, Chichester, two sections a day, for nearly two years and in March 1917 they received a letter of commendation from the Hospital Quartermaster, Lieutenant Colonel Kidd, who concluded with these words:

> 'I congratulate you on the excellent work the members of the Bognor Red Cross continue to render to the hospital, thus showing how thoroughly they are appreciated. The good discipline and high standard of work is entirely due to the Quartermaster, who also combines the duties of the Lady Superintendent and is untiring in her work, which requires constant thought and wise judgement.'

The Bognor Red Cross helped in the transfer of many hundreds of wounded and sick soldiers back to Graylingwell, very often the last leg of their journey being made in Ambulance Trains, one of which made a pre-service visit to Bognor.

> 'A new Ambulance Train, constructed by the London, Brighton and South Coast Railway, arrived at Bognor Railway Station prior to entering service, where over one thousand Bognorians inspected it, raising £51 11s towards the train's running costs.

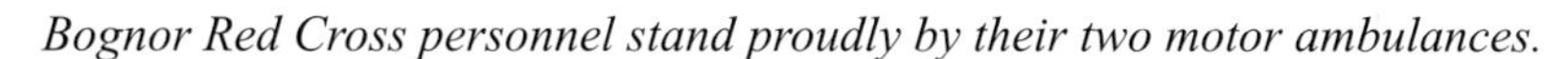

Bognor Red Cross personnel stand proudly by their two motor ambulances.

> The train was painted in khaki, with large red crosses on each side of the carriages. When operational it could carry one hundred and forty four stretcher cases fitted in tiers in the four 'ward cars', three hundred and twenty walking wounded in the five 'sitting cars' and had one carriage reserved for those suffering from an infectious disease. Emergency operations could be carried out in the pharmacy car, whilst two others were fitted as kitchen and catering cars. A Staff Car was also attached, plus two brake cars.'

The Women's Institute

The ever dependable ladies of the Women's Institute were quick to respond to the War effort, collecting and distributing articles of clothing for the soldiers at the Front, particularly shirts, drawers, vests, socks and gloves, from a distribution centre that was set up in London Road. A Soldiers and Sailors Welcome Club was formed by them in Waterloo Square, where gifts of eggs, lettuce and fruit, were 'gratefully received'. They also held a market each week, appealing for produce from allotment holders. They traded on a strictly 'cash only' basis, allotment holders and farmers finding it 'a good way for earning money from excess produce'. These products were then also despatched to the Front.

The Norman Thompson Flight Company

Nearby Middleton on Sea, with its large expanse of firm sand for possible use as a runway, attracted the attention of the engineer Norman Thompson in 1910, as being the ideal location for his fledgling aircraft company. Originally called the White and Thompson Aeronautical Engineer's following his partnership with a financier friend Douglas White, large hangars were erected and several aeroplanes were designed. Following a severe storm in 1913 which removed large amounts of sand, the Company turned to making seaplanes, acquiring a licence to service Glen Curtis's visiting flying boat from America. From this, White and Thompson acquired a further licence to build flying boats to the general Curtis design. Plans were made to enter two flying boats, based broadly on the Curtis principles but both of British design throughout, designated the White and Thompson No 1 and No 2 Flying Boats, in the Daily Mail 1914 Round Britain Race, but were cancelled due to the outbreak of war.

However, the Royal Naval Air Service took an interest in the Company, now renamed the Norman Thompson Flight Company Limited and soon orders were received for flying boats, which were used for U Boat patrols in the North Sea. An immediate need for more workers saw the Company expand from a dozen or so employees in 1914 to nearly 900 before the cessation of hostilities and a subsidiary, Williams and Company, on the banks of the River Arun in Littlehampton, was employed making flying boat hulls as well as high speed tender launches. Many Bognorians were employed, along with workers from the outlying districts who were bussed or transported by open lorry to work each day. In all the company produced well over 200 seaplanes for the Navy, but the signing of the Armistice was quickly followed by the cancellation of further aircraft and the Company soon went into liquidation.

Civilian Volunteers

The Hotham War Rooms were started to supply 'necessaries' for the hospitals. Some forty volunteer workers each week were engaged in making surgeons' overalls and caps, flannel bed jackets, capellines, operation stockings, socks, bed socks, flannel boots, abdominal and other bandages, operation sets, shell dressings, swabs and plugging of all kinds, resulting in over 5000 articles being sent in the first year. The scheme was funded by waste paper disposal. Some of the £400 and more raised by this method also supported the Red Cross.

The Women's Emergency Corps was formed, whose members would be regularly seen on the beach, filling sand bags to be sent to the Front - really heavy work.

A Bognor Voluntary Workers' Association, operating from Grosmont Preparatory School, 2 Sidlaw Terrace, Clarence Road, set to work making mufflers, socks, shirts, helmets, mittens and other comforts for the troops, for whom an appeal for 500 vests made of muslin was made on behalf of 4th Battalion The Royal Sussex Regiment. All goods were then despatched via Horsham; it was a well organized operation, 'the Bognor women are splendid', enthused the *Bognor Observer*.

The invalids of the Merchant Taylors Homes, sited in the north of Waterloo Square, also made shirts and pillows and collected books for the wounded being treated at the Graylingwell Military Hospital.

Carrying On

For some, life in Bognor during those first months of the war in 1914 was not that different: the 'season', following a short slump in numbers, picked up fairly well. Arthur Davies, for instance, having had his char-a-bancs requisitioned for troop movements early on, soon resumed his normal business:

> 'Mr Davies's splendid Commer motor char-a-bancs will make weekend trips to London and back during the rest of the season, besides journeys on Wednesday and Fridays to Southampton, Portsmouth and Brighton. The single fare to London is 5s and from London is the same, while the return fare to Portsmouth is 3s 6d, to Southampton, 7s 6d and Brighton 5s.
>
> In addition to these long runs, Mr Davies has arranged a large programme of interesting local drives and cars run daily to Arundel, Slindon and Chichester, taking in the most picturesque

Seen here in more peaceful days, the char-a-bancs of Arthur Davies, soon returned to their normal trade, after being requisitioned at the beginning of the war.

routes and affording passengers ample time to view the interesting buildings and beautiful scenery for which Sussex is famous. Visitors should not miss seeing Sussex in its summer glory from one of Davies's comfortable and commodious cars.'

However, other traders in the High Street and business men within the town were not so fortunate; thirty one of them, covering all aspects of the retail trade, appealed to the Bognor public to keep faith with them:

> 'The most serious problem of the moment, in the eyes of all business people of Bognor, is how to keep the people as far as possible fully employed. The reduction of staff, whether it is in the counting house, the workroom, or the factory, would be one of the worst evils which could befall the business community and the Town at large.
>
> If the public will help us by placing their orders and making their purchases as usual, they will also help to a much greater extent the large number of men and women engaged in the maintenance of our establishments and work rooms and the still larger number of people employed in the manufacture of the articles which we offer for sale.
>
> With the assistance of our customers we believe that it may be possible to maintain our regular Staffs. The inevitable difficulties of the situation will be greatly reduced if the Public realise the fact that the best way to safety is to alter their arrangements and habits of life as little as they can.'

Football

The reduction in men folk, of whom by the end of 1914 some 600 or so had enlisted, also affected sport, particularly football. At a pre season meeting of the West Sussex Football League, many clubs reported their inability to complete all their fixtures. Bognor Football Club had already lost six players to the Colours, including their star man A Holland, who had joined his Regiment, the Scots Guards and at least two more were likely to follow in the coming weeks. North Bersted Football Club was in a similar position, as were Chichester, who had lost nine players and Felpham and Yapton who 'have practically all their eleven in the Sussex Yeomanry'. The clubs were advised to 'rope off their pitches' if they were unable to play and the fixture list was severely curtailed, the season's fixtures not being completed.

....AND THE WAR FRONT

The members of the British Expeditionary Force started arriving in France on 9 August and by 22nd of the month some 160,000 men had been ferried across the Channel, closely chaperoned by the powerful Royal Navy. Compared to the large conscripted armies of most European countries the BEF was small in numbers, reportedly described by the Kaiser as 'a contemptible little army'. It was soon in action, firstly at Mons and Le Cateau, before taking part in the Great Retreat to the River Marne, where it successfully counter attacked. Boosted by reinforcements, further battles took place at the Aisne, in the Armentieres area and in the First Battle of Ypres. Casualties were high and the BEF suffered greatly, but its brave actions helped to contain the German advance and kept the vital Channel ports in allied hands. Fourteen Bognor soldiers lost their lives in the first five months of the war.

Meanwhile, the Royal Navy was in action, with ten Bognor sailors lost at sea, Able Seaman Frederick Woodland in an Australian submarine being the first. Others soon followed with the sinking by the German submarine U9 of HMS *Aboukir, Cressy* and *Hogue* whilst patrolling the North Sea and the loss of HMS *Good Hope* in the Battle of Coronel off the coast of Chile.

In the initial euphoria to sign up and 'fight the Hun' it was expected quite widely that it would be 'all over by Christmas'. But December 1914 presented a different picture, with many homes without their fathers and sons, away fighting, the whole town aware that twenty four men would never be returning.

The war was beginning to hit home. It was not going to be all over by Christmas.

CHAPTER 4

1915

War Front

In 1915 Captain Fairfax became the first local Royal Flying Corps casualty, killed when his aircraft crashed over Paris in January, whilst the submariner Able Seaman Irish was lost with his boat somewhere in the North Sea the same week. Until the end of April local casualties amounted to just seven. Numbers then increased dramatically with battles taking place involving local men at Neuve Chapelle, Ypres, Richebourg L'Avoue and Aubers Ridge in the later fighting, the Royal Sussex Regiment sustaining heavy casualties.

This letter appeared in the *Bognor Observer* in May 1915, written by an 'unknown Officer of the Regiment' and it refers to heavy losses in 2nd Battalion Royal Sussex Regiment. These occurred in the Battle of Aubers Ridge, fought on 9 May:

> 'We embarked on a desperate enterprise. By the merciful power of God I got through safely. I cannot say too much but there has never been such a day. After a bombardment by our guns on the German trenches, the good old Sussex went forward like one man, only to be met by a fire from the gunners which simply mowed our men down like rabbits. The barbed wire in front of the trenches was not cut by our shrapnel as had been planned and we were caught up like rats in a trap. I cannot express myself as I would like to, but it was perfect hell. We had fourteen Officer casualties and 580 men casualties. Luckily our Colonel was not touched, nor our Adjutant. Though we were unable to

> take the trenches and had to retire, we got through and all our men were heroes, for they enabled others to go through us and reap the honour and glory.
>
> 'What were left of the Sussex were sent back to have a rest. It had been hell let loose, the boys stuck to it and were mown down like corn. Well it is no good grieving about it. I know our dead heroes would not have us do that. We must pull ourselves together and wait for our reinforcements and get ready for another go, although we shall have to sacrifice many more lives yet to bring this horrid war to a finish and it would be far better to be dead than to be ruled by the German savages, for they cannot fight fairly. They have to poison us with their gasses, but there will be no more mercy shown to them now, for I can tell you the boys are longing to have another go at them.'

Casualty numbers rose again in September as the Battle of Loos raged across the Channel and the horrors of the Gallipolli campaign became known. Forty-nine local men lost their lives in 1915.

Local Hero

A Bognorian to gain recognition early in the war was Sergeant F Eade, of 1st Rifle Brigade, whose parents lived in Chapel Street. In March 1915 he gained promotion to Sergeant from Private for 'gallantry in the field'. Then in September he received four separate congratulatory intimations from the General Officer Commanding the Division that he had been noticed by his Commanding Officer for 'conspicuous bravery in the field', and was mentioned twice in despatches, once by Field Marshal Sir John French, Commander-in-Chief of the British Expeditionary Force and then by Sir Douglas Haig, at that time Commander of the British First Army. Two years later he was awarded the Military Medal.

Recruitment

In the cold light of the New Year it became obvious that the war was not going to be over as quickly as had been originally anticipated. Recruitment was continuing, but as the spring approached there were signs that the numbers of volunteers were slowing down, despite recruitment meetings and appeals in the local press.

The initial enthusiasm was over and with casualties back home, their lives and bodies shattered, minus arms, legs, some blinded, others mentally disturbed, volunteer recruiting numbers fell. Each week in local papers the list of those who had made the supreme sacrifice also increased in length, but the Government's demand for more men continued unabated. More Bognor volunteers were now required. In order to alleviate doubts in the minds of the prospective recruits, one Recruiting Officer at a rally in the Queens Hall, said:

> 'If a soldier is shot at six in the morning, he will be in bed in by six in the evening. Once he is in the ambulance train he will be hurried through to the base hospital. The wounded will be on stretchers and every effort will be made to get them back as quickly as possible.'

The War Office also authorized the raising of another Battalion of Sussex Territorials for home defence, as many had waived their option of not serving abroad, although this possibility was clearly still being used to raise recruits.

> 'Those in Bognor who had hitherto been dissuaded from joining the Army, by mothers, grandmothers or sweethearts, now have their chance, an opportunity of joining a Reserve Battalion, as the chances are a million to one that they will not be bought against the Germans.'

With further Territorials departing Newhaven to go 'elsewhere' in April 1915, 'their departure being witnessed by great crowds' the pressure was on to fill their places. Major BT Hodgson, the Commanding Officer of the newly forming Territorial Battalion, issued a press release the following month:

> 'I desire to draw the attention of the men from Chichester, Bognor, Littlehampton and neighbourhood over the age of enlistment, who have not yet joined some branch of His Majesty's Forces, to the urgent need of recruits to 4th Battalion Royal Sussex Territorial Third Unit which I am now raising. This, the local Battalion, should have the universal support of the men of this district, whereas I fear that several men are being drawn off to other units not connected with the County. In order to supply drafts to our 1st Battalion when it goes abroad I have to raise between 500 and 600 men and to do this I must have the hearty co-operation of West Sussex. I feel sure that when the facts are known, every man in the district will feel that it is his paramount duty to make sure that his County Territorial Unit has all the men it needs.'

At yet another recruiting meeting at the Queens Hall, the visiting Recruiting Officer stated:

> 'Bognor has done its bit, now I am going to urge that Bognor does a bit more. If a boy is just under seventeen, but feels like seventeen, let him go. And if some are just over the age limit, they should say they have lost their birth certificates. Wives should let their husbands go and if they don't come back, well, they'll have a noble death.'

Signs, perhaps, of concern that recruiting might be tailing off, but response was slow and a further newspaper appeal was made, this time with a veiled threat:

> 'Recently, we have not had a single recruit from the Bognor district and that does not seem right. I know how well Bognor has done during the past few months, but I would appeal for her to do still better. In the Battalion that is going abroad there are between 50 and 60 men from Bognor and Felpham and I feel sure that Bognor and Felpham will not let them go without the satisfaction of knowing that a Reserve of their own friends is in training to come out to their assistance. Every village in the area is to be systematically searched. Town areas deserve more

> careful attention as in proportion they do not seem to have produced as good results as the country and there must be a very large number of men who have not come forward yet. Signs are that some form of compulsion will soon be adopted and there is no doubt that then a great difference will be made between men who have 'volunteered' and those who will have to be 'fetched'.

The Derby Scheme

It was now clear that the numbers required were not going to be sustained despite the upper age limit being raised from 38 to 40 in May 1915. The Government passed the National Registration Act in July, aimed at discovering how many men between the ages of 15 and 65 were engaged in a particular trade. Apart from those who were already in the military, who were exempted, all others were obliged to register their employment details. The results, when announced in September, revealed there were almost five million men of military age, around one and a half million of whom were in protected or 'starred' occupations, leaving many eligible for military service. The Government, reluctant to introduce conscription, opted for a halfway house system and enlisted the services of Lord Derby, who had already played a major part in raising volunteers. He was given the title of Director-General of Recruiting and introduced his 'Derby Scheme' for increasing numbers, in which men were told that they could continue to volunteer, or 'attest' with an obligation to come forward when called. In the meantime they returned to their homes and jobs, sporting a grey armband with a red crown emblazoned on it as a sign that they had volunteered, thus avoiding any insulting white feather incidents.

An appeal went out for men over military age to 'undertake the difficult and responsible work of canvassing', which commenced in Bognor in November. Canvassers were issued with cards which were filled out at every house visited in the Bognor district to 'encourage men to attest': those who agreed were issued with their Derby Armlets at Bognor Police Station.

> 'The greatest interest and not a little concern in some quarters is being everywhere manifested in Lord Derby's scheme for enlisting recruits, although there are problems getting enough canvassers.'

Attested men were trained whilst still civilians, attending at the Bedford Street Drill Hall two or three evenings a week, with 'musketry training every Saturday evening at 7pm'.

> 'As civilians it will help them overcome the irksome recruit stage, enable them to become physically fit and prevent any undue strain when called up. It will be of great assistance in securing rapid and early promotion when they join the Colours.'

Even so, not everybody was happy because some men, although having attested and been accepted, found that by visiting a local civilian doctor they could be declared unfit. The ruse was made public by one Derby recruit in a letter to the *Bognor Observer*:

> 'I am a young Derby recruit who has not yet been called up and I am writing to ask you if you would be good enough to put in your correspondence column what I think is not fair to those of us who have come forward to do our bit. I am alluding to the medical examination. Towards the end of the period for attestation under Lord Derby's scheme there were crowds at the York Road office and I with many others were lightly examined and passed fit. We were then sworn in and some of us have had our 2s 9d but others have not had theirs yet. There seems to have been some muddle. But since then I have found out that a good many who I thought would be in the Army with me have been passed as unfit. What they tell me they did was to go to the Doctor's house and ask him to examine them privately and after telling them the tale they then found out they were unfit, but they cannot actually tell me what is wrong with them. I am not complaining about the Sergeant Major who gave us all the information we wanted, but I do complain that it is not playing the game to go up to the Doctors house and get a special examination. The fairest way I can see is for all those who have been rejected by the Doctor to go before the Army Doctor at the Chichester Barracks. I think before anybody is given an 'unfit' armlet they should be examined again to see if their complaints are bad enough to reject them from military service.

'Hoping you will be able to find room for this and thanking you in anticipation.

'A willing Derby Recruit.'

By June 1915 the numbers of those serving in the Army or Navy accounted for 18% of the entire male population of Bognor District and not a single playing member of the North Bersted Football Club was left at home. The North Bersted Band had also ceased to function as the majority of the bandsmen had either volunteered or re-enlisted.

Not only soldiers were recruited. The state of the roads at the Front made it difficult for the military and its equipment to travel and an appeal went out for volunteer civilian labour:

'The Bognor Surveyor is energetically organising the labour that can be spared from the Bognor District for service in France in reconstructing the roads, which have been seriously damaged by the excessive traffic they have to bear. The wages offered to men over military age is 3s 0d a day, with food, housing and a separation allowance for the wives and families that have been

By mid-1915 all the eligible members of the North Bersted Band had enlisted.

left behind of 1s 8d per day. Several drafts have already left the town for Bordon Camp where the men are being fitted out before going to France to help in making 'the great roads to victory'. Who will volunteer? Men are still wanted.'

The wage offered was very good; more than a fighting soldier was being paid.

Wounded Soldiers

Wounded soldiers back home recovering from injuries were becoming a familiar sight and naturally people wished to speak to them about their experiences and injuries. This approach was not always welcome as the *Bognor Observer* commented:

'Some people have such a senseless idea of expressing their sympathy when meeting someone wounded home from the Front. When you meet a wounded Tommy it is generally the reverse of kindness to make him talk of his wounds and how he received them and the small chance he may have of a complete recovery. The best sympathy is cheerfulness and a hopeful spirit supplemented where possible by a little tangible comfort.'

Invasion Fears and Zeppelins

There were still fears of a possible German invasion; the refugees from Belgium were, of course, a reminder that England could suffer the same fate. Plans for the necessary actions had been made should an invasion of the United Kingdom take place, but were kept secret until January 1915, when they were published in the local press, having been issued by the Duke of Norfolk, as Lord Lieutenant of Sussex:

'If the invasion comes, until now great secrecy has been observed in regard to the arrangements which have been made to the civil population as to the course they should follow should any landing of the enemy be made on our shores. That such a landing should take place the action to be taken by the civilian population are the removal and destruction of everything which might be of use to the invading forces, such as horses, stock, food and vehicles. No civilian may have recourse to the use of

Airship over The Steyne, Bognor.

> firearms or other weapons against an invading enemy, except under certain conditions to be announced at the time.'

The numbers of Special Constables had risen to nearly 200, many of whom were called upon on the evening of 15 April when a warning was received that a Zeppelin was approaching Bognor from across the Channel. Immediately the air raid plan was put into action, the public being warned by the lowering, raising and lowering again of the gas pressure, there usually being a considerable quantity of gas in the pipes; the Specials also attended to the turning out of the street lamps and oil lamps that were considered dangerous.

The Special Constables' Section Commanders also turned out under the watchful eye of Colonel Fryer and the Fire Brigade and Red Cross also stood by all night, ready for any emergency. However, all was well, the Zeppelin turned eastwards and launched an attack on East Sussex. As an 'exercise' the evening had been successful, according to the *Bognor Observer*:

> 'The whole thing was carried out in such a manner as to bring credit to all concerned, being also of considerable value as a practical experiment for the real thing, if and when it comes.'

On His Majesty's Service.

NOTICE TO HOUSEHOLDERS.

Instructions in case of Bombardment or Air-raid.

Though it is *most improbable* that an attack of any sort will be made by the enemy in the neighbourhood of Bognor, yet it is thought best as a matter of precaution to issue certain instructions,

In the event of any sort of attack the Government strongly advise the inhabitants to remain in their houses and where possible to take shelter in cellars or basements.

Occupants of houses actually on the sea-front should in case of a bombardment leave their houses by the back-door and take shelter elsewhere.

Unexploded shells or bombs should not be touched as they are liable to explode if moved. The Police or Military Authorities should be informed where they are.

No persons, except those on duty, should remain in the streets.

The gas and electric light will probably be turned off at the main. People using gas should turn it off at the jet, and everyone should keep a stock of candles by them.

Instructions in case of a state of emergency caused by a threatened landing of the enemy.

1.—*Warning* of an impending attack will be given by the firing of maroons.

2.—*Persons* who may wish to leave the district must do so immediately that the signal is given. The only road which will be available will be the road from Bognor to Westergate. Other roads must not be used as they will be required by the Military.

3.—*If* troops are met on any roads civilians must take to the fields and leave the road clear until the Military have passed.

4.—*The* population of outlying or solitary houses are strongly advised to go at once into the Towns or larger villages.

5.—*All* persons owning bicycles which in the case of an emergency they do not intend to use, should at once disable them to avoid their being used by the enemy.

6.—*In* no case must there be any attempt at resistance by civilians either with fire-arms or otherwise. Any such attempt might bring the most terrible consequences on the whole district.

The Civil population must promptly obey all instructions given by the Military, Police or Special Constables.

Signed,

H. H. GIBBS,
Chairman, Bognor Urban District Council.

H. D. FRYER, Colonel,
Member of Emergency Committee
Chichester Petty Sessional Division.

JOHN HAVILAND,
Head Special Constable, In charge of Civil Population.

Webster & Webb, Printers and Stationers, High Street, Bognor.

Lighting Restrictions

Lighting restrictions were introduced soon after, firstly as a trial:

> 'The past week has been significant for the public orders which have been issued with regard to lights', commented the *Bognor Observer*. 'As we were about to go to press with our last issue an order came for all lights to be extinguished which could be seen from outside. Consequently on Tuesday evening our town was in almost total darkness, but thanks to the moon, the inconvenience was not half as bad as it might have been.

On Wednesday there was quite a boom in the sale of dark coloured blinds, while numberless people searched their store cupboards for old curtains or anything else which would serve to shut interior illumination from the outside world. The efforts to secure complete darkness were therefore nearer perfection on Wednesday, but on Thursday there came the welcome news that the order had been rescinded. Whilst most people are hoping that no such order will again be deemed necessary in the interests of public safety, a word of praise is due to the Police, Special Constables and the Boy Scouts, for the expeditious manner in which they performed their duty of notifying the public of what was required of them.'

The Lighting Order, however, was soon in force and throughout the duration of the war several hundred Bognorians found themselves in court on charges of showing too much light, fines of up to forty shillings being commonplace. Here are some early examples:

'Three cases under the Lighting Order for not obscuring indoor lights, so as to be invisible from the outside, came before His Grace, the Duke of Richmond and Gordon KG., and other Magistrates at the Chichester County Petty Sessions on Saturday.

The first defendant was Henry Harman Newell, the licensee of the Bedford Hotel, Bognor, who pleaded not guilty.

Inspector Bristow said at 10.35pm on 22 April he saw a very bright light showing south-west. He had difficulty in finding the light because it came through a lot of chimneys and houses. He eventually went to the Bedford Hotel. The light kept going up and down for several minutes, but he could tell it was not semaphore signalling. He told the defendant the light was coming from the back of his hotel, the defendant treated the matter very lightly and as the servants had gone to bed in the room referred to he called again the next morning. There was no blind in the window and from the room he could see the sea.

By the defendant: He was not on the seafront and it was possible that the light could not be seen from there. He could see the sea from the window, but he could not get a boat to go to sea to see if he could see the window from the sea (laughter).

> This window is 2 feet 7 inches by 2 feet 9 inches, with six squares of glass and from the seafront you cannot see two squares.'

Special Constable Benham corroborated.

The defendant told the Bench that two girls slept in this room. One went to bed first and after she had put her candle out she took the blind down, forgetting the other girl, who went to bed without replacing it. He had given the girls particular instructions to have all lights subdued. He could not go into the girl's bedroom every night to see if the lights were out.

The Duke told him he would be fined 40 shillings; 'you must take steps to see the lights are obscured. I don't see the reason for a personal visit each evening to see that the lights are out.'

Defendant: 'It's rather hard when one tries to do his best.'

The second defendant was Albert Ide of West Street, who pleaded guilty.

Special Constable Edwards said that at 9.00pm on 3 May he saw a light coming from the defendant's shop, the explanation was given that they had forgotten to put up the blind. The light was visible from the sea.

The defendant said he had left the premises at the time and his man, who wished to finish some work, forgot to put up the blind. It was quite unintentional.

Albert Ide was also fined 40 shillings.

The last defendant was Charles Johnson, who wrote to the Court to say he was very sorry.

Inspector Bristow said the light came from the back of the defendant's premises at 11.00pm. There was no blind and the light was very bright. He sent a Constable to the house and waited himself until the light was taken away.

In his letter the defendant stated that the light was in the bathroom window and the fault lay with the tenant. Fined 40 shillings, the Chairman remarked that the defendant had better tell his tenants to bath in the mornings (laughter).

Large numbers of persons summoned to appear to answer for lighting offences failed to attend, either answering by post or ignoring the summons completely, so much so that the Chichester County Bench issued an edict warning defendants. The previous week only three defendants out of over twenty cases bothered to attend.

> 'If defendants do not appear then their cases will be adjourned for a fortnight and then failure to attend will result in warrants being issued for their apprehension. Whatever views may be held of the wisdom of the Lighting Regulations, or the methods adopted by the Police in carrying them into effect, courtesy at least is due to the Magistrates from those who are summoned. The Chichester County Bench has been too lenient in the past in overlooking the absence of the majority of the offenders against whom proceedings have been taken.'

Cricket

The summer of 1915 saw cricket being affected by the war for the first time. County cricket matches had already been cancelled for the season, with so many players 'with the Colours'. Now Bognor Cricket Club faced the same problem. At the pre season AGM the matter was discussed at length, the meeting acknowledging that only a few matches amongst schoolboys would be possible in August, 'when the schools had broken up'. Their main problem was the upkeep of the Nyewood Lane ground, which if neglected 'would take a very long time to recover'. Funds to maintain the ground were also going to be low as many subscribers were at the Front, although several at the meeting 'signified their intention of doubling their last year's subscriptions to make up the shortfall'. With that the meeting closed, no cricket would be played in 1915, the members hoping to resume a normal programme the following year.

The Southdowns

Some of the local volunteers returned to Bognor for a weekend as part of 11th (Southdown) Battalion Band, The Royal Sussex Regiment.

> 'Bognorians manifested a lively interest in a visit of the Band of their newly formed 11th Southdowns Battalion, the Royal Sussex Regiment, which came to Bognor for a weekend visit, which was interesting as many of its recruits came from Bognor, thanks to the efforts of Captain Grisewood (the son of Lt Col

Grisewood) and also the father of the Bognor Boys, Sergeant Major G E May who, although a veteran, had enlisted into the Southdowns.

'The Band consisted of 60 members and they arrived at 5.00pm, marching to the Western Bandstand, where they gave a short programme of music to the enjoyment of a large crowd. They were subsequently entertained to high tea at Walls Restaurant by the Urban Council. In the evening the announcement that they would appear at the Pier Theatre to give a programme of music in connection with the picture entertainment drew a large crowd and the various items were enthusiastically applauded and encored, their performances manifesting in a high standard of proficiency, considering that they had not been embodied very long. On Sunday morning the band gave a performance at the Den, the residence of Mrs Grisewood which attracted a large concourse of people, while in the evening they gave a popular selection of music at the Kursaal Rink which drew a large crowd.'

(This was to be Sergeant Major May's last duty after a long and successful military career. He became ill a day or two later and died.)

Military Bands

The subject of military bands and their availability was to exercise the Town Council as they debated the programme for the 1915 season, which covered the months of July and August. Traditionally, various military bands were booked to give concerts in both bandstands and on the Pier. Now with the war raging across the Channel there was some concern as to which bands were available, whilst others took the line that no bands should be booked during the conflict. After much discussion and press coverage the Council decided to go ahead and 'book' as normal, accepting whichever bands were available and a full programme went ahead.

Defence of the Realm

Being a coastal town, photography in certain places was restricted; 'to have in one's possession photographic equipment in a public place without lawful authority' attracted frequent prosecutions. The taking of photographs was banned on the sea front and various other places and was an unpopular move, with those caught breaking the rules fined on average ten shillings each for using a camera without authority. A visitor to Pagham fared even worse:

> 'A young visitor to Pagham was summoned for having in his possession a photographic apparatus without lawful authority. The Chief Officer of the Coastguard at Felpham said he was going towards Pagham in a military transport when he saw the defendant in the act of taking a photo. He got down and told him he was in a restricted area and could not use it, a female who was with him said that it was 'a lot of rot'. He was fined 20 shillings.'

The photographic ban was more serious for one man. William Ashton of Kentura House, Highfield Road, 'the well known beach photographer, is prohibited by the Naval and Police authorities from continuing to carry out his profession on the sand. As Mr Ashton's family depend on him and he is bordering fifty years of age, this action comes as a great hardship to him.'

Home Front

For the general public, help was required in a more unusual way. They were told to smoke more, the *Bognor Observer* supporting the scheme:

> 'Smoke more not less, smoking is a duty, for every one shilling paid for tobacco half goes in tax. The revenue is required as the sinews of war. Smoking is a patriotic action because it helps strengthen the finances of the country.'

The newspaper also appealed for cash to provide more tobacco for the troops:

> 'Every sixpence received by the *Bognor Observer* will pay for thirty five cigarettes, two ounces of tobacco and one packet of matches. If purchased in the ordinary way this would cost one shilling and sixpence.'

Fresh eggs were also required for the troops to the tune of some 200,000 per week nationally. Collecting points were set up in Bognor and the *Bognor Observer* published the totals donated, usually approaching 2000 per week. An 'egg skating rink carnival' was held at the Kursaal and raised the cost of 1000 eggs in a single day. A Mrs Gibbs was placed in charge of the Bognor sub depot of the National Egg Collection and by June 1915, 6881 eggs had been forwarded for the benefit of wounded sailors and soldiers. With the opening of the Graylingwell War Hospital in March 1915 a further 500 eggs a week were sent there.

Mrs Walters of the White Tower, Aldwick Road, Bognor, who collected and despatched clean shirts to men at the Front, made an appeal in the *Bognor Observer*:

> 'Perhaps some gentlemen of the neighbourhood can find one or two suitable shirts in their wardrobes, also small sums towards their postage would be useful. Colonel Hayes has given me five shillings and Mrs Hayes two shillings, apart from that I have paid all the postage and for the cigarettes myself. I may add that one poor man bought me a new shirt and intimated that he would try to do something once a month. Perhaps others might follow his example.'

Food donations to the soldiers also became very important, with a distribution centre established at 3 London Road, Bognor. Concerns that the prisoners of war were not being fed properly led to another newspaper appeal:

> 'When you are shopping, please remember the prisoners of war', was the call, as many Bognorians rallied round, sending cocoa, soup packets and tinned meat.

First Anniversary Church Services

In June 1915 a service was held at St John's Church for the fallen of Bognor:

> 'Few people in Bognor will remember seeing such a great congregation as filled the Parish church on Sunday 13 June at a special Memorial Service for those who had lost their lives in

The Kursaal, a popular venue, with its skating rink and meeting point for soldiers on leave.

> the war. The congregation was so large that it stretched right out into the road.'

The first anniversary of the war service for Bognor was also held at St John's Parish Church on a Wednesday afternoon in August. Being half day closing, a large number of residents were able to attend; 'even the seating accommodation of the Lady Chapel had to be requisitioned'. The military stationed in the vicinity also paraded to hear 'a stirring address' by the Vicar, the Reverend JJ Priestly. Sadly, this was to be his last service, as three days later he died in his sleep.

Another service was held at South Bersted Church, which was crowded to capacity, the Church Lads' Brigade and Band paraded and the Last Post was played by Private C Chuter.

In his address the Reverend F T P Evershed paid tribute to the nine men from the Parish who had fallen during the last twelve months:

> 'Of the Navy men, one had gone down in a submarine in Australian Seas and another in a submarine elsewhere, site unknown. One had gone down in HMS *Aboukir* off the English East Coast and a fourth had perished with HMS *Good Hope* off the west coast of South America.
>
> Of the Army men the first to fall had died in the Great Retreat when the German hordes pressed so heavily on the small British Expeditionary Force then in the field. The others had been shot in the trenches. Of the five Army men, three had received their schooling in the Parish School next to the Church.'

The Summer Season

At the end of the summer the *Bognor Observer* announced that despite the war it had been a record season:

> 'It is an obvious fact that despite the great world war, the season at Bognor will be a record one in regards to numbers of visitors requiring apartments. The long stretch of golden sands were fully occupied by families who came for a fortnight or month's holiday. The weekend for Bank Holiday saw a great influx of visitors and enquiries at the railway station elicited the response that the weekend had beaten all records.

> The tradesmen, with their war depleted staffs, are possibly working harder than they have ever done to cope with the catering of the population, three or four times the normal aggregate. Many people foolishly came down with their luggage to find apartments and had to leave the place unsuccessful. Bank Holiday was unfortunately very stormy with rain setting in during the afternoon, which drove the people indoors to the profit of the amusement caterers, all the places of entertainment being filled afternoon and evening.'

Entertaining the Wounded Soldiers of Graylingwell War Hospital

Apart from the medical care, wounded soldiers at Graylingwell received a large amount of volunteer support from the residents of Bognor. Regular cinematography shows took place, seaside vaudeville entertainers travelled from as far as Southsea, many of the Bognor entertainers played regularly there, as did a theatre group from Arundel. A support group received gifts and monetary donations throughout the war and every Christmas the local papers contained lists of those who donated presents for the inmates.

Among the many individual residents who 'did their bit' for the war effort were the Loibl sisters from Pagham, who formed a Concert Party in 1915 and gave open air entertainment, complete with a piano and harmonium, from the back of a lorry parked on the Esplanade and various other areas of the town. Monies raised bought little luxuries for the wounded soldiers at Graylingwell Military Hospital. The management of the Norfolk Hotel hosted a concert there which raised £5 19s 4d and Mr T Raynes, of Fernley, Victoria Drive, hosted fifty wounded soldiers from Graylingwell for tea, in 1915:

> 'They arrived at two o'clock and were provided with light refreshments. Some then paid a visit to the Kursaal, whilst others were entertained by the boatmen and enjoyed a bathe. Tea was served at five, a photo was taken and then they were entertained by Mr Hazel of the Olympian Gardens. They left at seven o'clock.'

Other residents took delight in giving wounded soldiers trips out in their motor cars to see the countryside and take the air:

Mr and Mrs Harris of Westholme, Victoria Road, Bognor (arrowed). organised motor trips for wounded soldiers recovering at Graylingwell Hospital, pictured here outside the Queen's Hall. The driver of the front car is Alfred Hampton, who enlisted soon afterwards in the Royal Army Service Corps.

> 'A small committee has been formed for the purpose of arranging motor trips for the wounded soldiers. The general idea is to have six or eight cars every Tuesday and Thursday to take the soldiers for short runs and it is hoped that the residents in the neighbourhood will assist in the movement by providing teas on one or more days.'

The sight of vehicles carrying wounded soldiers wearing their hospital blue uniforms was quite common until petrol shortages curtailed this somewhat.

Wives and Children

The South Bersted Committee of the Bognor Division of the Soldiers' and Sailors' Families Association looked after and entertained the wives and children of those who had gone to war, giving them a Christmas Party in December 1915:

> 'The children of over 100 servicemen gathered round the heavily laden tables, a sight not to be forgotten. After tea to the great delight of the children were revealed two huge Christmas trees which had been treated most abundantly with the contents of Father Christmas's sack. One by one the children were blessed with such articles as to bring delight to their young hearts. The National Anthem was sung with great gusto at the end.'

It was now the end of the first complete year of war, a year in which another fifty-eight local men had paid the supreme sacrifice.

CHAPTER 5

1916

War Front

January 1916 saw the completion of the withdrawal from Gallipolli which had commenced at the end of 1915.

In Europe local casualties in the first few months were thankfully low until the Battle of Jutland, when the British Grand Fleet and the German High Seas Fleet clashed in the North Sea at the Battle of Jutland. The *Bognor Observer* of 7 June 1916 reported:

> 'Eleven Bognor sailors were involved in the battle on various ships, eight of whom lost their lives. Another Bognor sailor lost his life the same week when HMS *Hampshire*, carrying Lord Kitchener for talks with the Russians, was lost.'

The casualty count rose even further from June with the Battle of the Somme, which lasted into the winter months. Seventy-nine local men lost their lives in 1916.

Local Hero

Private, later Sergeant Bailey, the son of Mr E Bailey, was born at the Homestead, North Bersted and had been a farm worker employed by John Harrison of Aldwick, enlisting at the outbreak of war when he was 17. He was medically discharged from the Army in August 1916, having been awarded the Military Medal. His bravery was recognized by Bersted Parish Council, who presented him with a gold watch and ten War Savings Certificates. The presentation was made at the Bersted

School, in North Bersted Street, which had been decorated for the occasion. The 'large company' gave Sergeant Bailey 'three rousing cheers' as he entered the room where a few short years earlier he had been a schoolboy, his presentation being made by his old schoolteacher.

His citation was as follows:

> 'Private Bailey had formed one of the bombing squad and assisted the Corporal to build a barricade in the enemy trench to block it. This was done under grenade and rifle fire. Their supply of bombs ran short and Private Bailey made three journeys into No Man's Land to collect bombs from the bodies of the fallen, these journeys being made under a heavy shell fire. He returned each time with bombs and threw at least fifty with good effect.'

His schoolteacher said:

> 'I congratulate you on winning the Military Medal and sympathize with you on your injury. I ask you to accept this watch and ten War Savings Certificates as a slight token of our appreciation and gratitude to you, may you long be spared to wear the watch. When you were one of my pupils in this school, I always found you a bright, intelligent and good boy. I feel sure that in the future you will not only be a credit to your family and North Bersted, but also your country.'

Sergeant Bailey replied:

> 'I am glad of the interest you are paying to me and I shall value the presents you have given me tonight more than anything else I possess'.

And with the audience singing 'For He's a Jolly Good Fellow', 19 year old Sergeant Bailey picked up his crutches and left the building, to face the rest of his life minus his right leg.

Recruitment

Meanwhile the Derby Scheme of recruitment had proved not to be a resounding success and was soon terminated, the last of the 'attested' men being called up in March 1916:

> 'The Barracks at Chichester saw something of a recruiting boom as men came to join the Colours. Some came in twos and threes, others as a score or more. Everything was done to make the men comfortable in their new surroundings.'

In January 1916 the Government had ushered in its long expected policy of Compulsory Service or Conscription for all unmarried men aged from 18 to 41. All voluntary recruitment ceased, including the Territorial Force; from now on every unmarried man, or a widower without dependants, was deemed to be in the Reserve, therefore eligible for war service and could be enlisted into any unit as directed by the military. Conscripts would receive a call up notice instructing them to report on a specific day at a named Recruiting Office and a Railway Warrant to ensure that they could get there.

In May the scheme was extended to include married men. There were of course exemptions, those whose civilian profession or trade were considered essential or indispensible, or whose call up would cause hardship to the family dependent on him, and conscientious objectors. Exemptions were not automatic, the applicant having to undergo an interview or series of interviews with a Tribunal, which could be daunting. Suspicions that there were men of certain professions, such as acting, who were avoiding the call up because of their 'nomadic' life style, resulted in raids on theatres.

> 'Police and military have been busy at Bognor raiding the stage at both the Kursaal and Pier Theatres, the actors being questioned as to their position under the Military Service Act. They carried out their raids with tact and discretion, one man was sent for a medical but found to be exempted and allowed to return to his theatrical company.'

Appeals

The Bognor Appeal Tribunal was constituted in January 1916 to consider the cases of men who applied for exemption from conscription. The Tribunal consisted at various times of several town worthies, a JP, a Recruiting Officer and a Military Representative. Applicants would appear and present their cases and receive the Tribunal's decision. These could vary from total exemption to immediate call up, or a period of time to attend to personal or business matters before being called. An appeals procedure was also available. These Tribunals were to continue until the end of the war, with many hundreds of local men attending them. Below are a few cases taken at random, from the *Bognor Observer*, their reports never revealing the applicant's name:

> 'A South Bersted resident aged 26, employed as a bread baker, applied for exemption on the grounds that in the event of enlistment serious hardship would ensue. The applicant said he was employed from 5.30am to 11.00am and also in the evenings making the sponge. He made the bread throughout the process and was the only one in the bake house who did and he had done it for fourteen years. He also did a small round, but did not consider himself a rounds man. His fellow employees were a van man, who knew nothing about bread making and an old man of 65, who was unreliable. His employer assisted in the bake house, but if he were laid up he would have to take it over.
>
> A letter from the employer stated that through the enlistment of six men he had had to close one shop and if the present applicant went he would have to close this one too.
>
> Lieutenant Marshal (Military Representative) suggested that women might be trained for the work, but a member of the Tribunal, who claimed experience, said this was beyond women's work.'

The applicant was given two months exemption from call up.

In another example a man engaged in collecting Income Tax in Bognor claimed exemption on the grounds that 'collecting Taxes was expedient in the national interest and that he should be allowed to continue in his present employment. But his application was only made for conditional exemption until the present tax year was completed. The applicant explained that he had had nine years training on Income

Tax work and it would take two years to train a substitute, if one could be found. His work this year was more difficult than ever before and the workload had greatly increased, he was working overtime every night, but still his collections were in arrears.'

His application was supported by the 'Government authorities and the Surveyor of Taxes', but it made little difference. He was given a three months exemption only.

Sometimes an applicant claimed exemption on medical grounds, as did this next case, a man who worked in a local cinema as the operator. Living with his widowed mother, he was supporting her to the tune of £1 per week out of his wages of £1 15s 0d. His brother had joined up, but he was medically fit, whilst the applicant had had to give up the job of a stage carpenter in London because of his condition. His case was postponed for a fortnight during which time the applicant had to undergo a medical examination.

Applications were often refused at the first hearing, as in this case of a fishmonger and poulterer who applied for a three month exemption for an employee 'in the national interest'. The employee also did all the buying, killing and preparing of his poultry. When asked if he could not do the buying himself, he replied that he did not understand poultry and he could not do the killing because 'he hadn't got the heart to'!

Conscientious Objectors

Others claimed exemption on the grounds of conscience, citing religious beliefs, anti-war pacifism and others who refused to accept that Germany was Britain's enemy. Some were prepared to do non fighting duties as stretcher bearers or work in munitions factories and all had to argue their case at a Tribunal.

Conscientious Objectors were not generally well received, but many stood by their principles in the face of some tough questioning by the Tribunal members. Those attending Tribunals were given leave to appeal after their initial appearance, which was made locally. These would be at County level, where the Military Representative would also have the right of appeal if he thought the applicant had got 'too much of the deal'. If the appeal went to its third stage this would be at National level, as there was only one Central Tribunal sitting in the United Kingdom. There were many appeals in Bognor and here we will 'sit in' on a couple – only their Christian names are divulged:

At one Tribunal William —— declared that he would have:

> 'Nothing whatsoever to do with this war, I have a conviction that it is wrong altogether and I shall stand by my conviction whatever you do.' The Tribunal gave him short shrift, fining him £2 and handing him over to the military. Men thus treated would then be escorted away from the Tribunal, others went on to appeal.

Nelson ——, was 28 years old, a foreman builder, who also looked after the accounts of a working men's club, as well as being an undertaker's assistant. He claimed exemption on the grounds of his 'objection to combatant service', because it was 'repulsive to his nature'. His Tribunal hearing included a certain amount of ridicule.

'He objects to killing them, but not burying them', opened the Chairman, amidst laughter from the Tribunal members; then addressing Nelson he asked,

> 'What is your conscientious objection?'
> 'Because I feel I could not do it, it would be against my nature.'
> 'Have you ever killed a rabbit or a rat?'
> 'Never.'
> 'Is it not on religious grounds that you object?'
> 'Anything of that kind would be repulsive to me.'
> 'Are you a vegetarian?'
> 'No.'
> 'Do you eat meat that others have killed?'
> 'Seldom, I never eat a lot.'

The Chairman then changed his line of questioning:

> 'If a young man assaulted your young lady what would you do?'
> 'I don't know what I should do.'
> 'You are not then setting up a conscientious objection on religious or moral grounds, but it is merely a question of repulsion to the shedding blood?'
> 'Not particularly.'
> 'You don't object to benefitting from the shedding of blood from anyone else. Men are dying for you at the Front and you are

going on living here at the expense of other men shedding their blood?'

'I don't think about it.'

'You've already told us that you object to the killing of a rabbit or rat, but you think it's alright to eat meat that someone else had killed?'

'I dislike the thought of killing anything.'

'Have you ever killed anything as a boy?'

'No.'

'Not killed a fly on a window pane?' (Laughter)

Nelson made no answer.

The Military Officer then took over the questioning and asked if he belonged to any religious body.

'I'm a non conformist.'

'Any particular religion?'

'No, nothing in particular.'

'Do you attend a place of worship?'

'Sometimes I go to the Wesleyan and sometimes to the Baptists.'

'There are a good many Wesleyan and Baptists at the Front doing their duty right now. Their religious leaders have spoken in favour of military service in the circumstances of war and they have gone there to minister for them. Do you ever read about the battles in the papers?'

'Yes I do.'

'You have read about the outrages that the Germans have committed on Belgium women who are always regarded as sacred?'

'Not particularly.'

'But you have read these outrages?'

'Yes.'

'You know the Germans have said that if they come over here they would act very much worse and commit the same outrages on our womenfolk. Don't you feel you are justified in taking action to prevent that occurring?'

'I should not care to take combative action.'

'What other action could you take?' demanded the Military Officer, to which Nelson made no answer.

He was asked to retire whilst the Tribunal discussed his objection, very soon deciding to refuse his exemption as his application 'did not rest on religious or moral convictions'.

Nelson appealed, which was heard a week later, this time accompanied by his father who spoke on his behalf, but to no avail. The appeal was refused and Nelson was informed that 'the Depot will take you within ten days'.

The Tribunals went on. A hurdle maker, whose religious beliefs were very strong, quoted from the Bible, St Matthew, 'all that take up the sword shall perish by the sword'. He objected to non combatant service as he could not see the difference between it and combatant service. He would not resort to the use of arms in any dispute. When asked if he would be willing to save a man's life, he said he would not take part in any military service, as it was all working for the same purpose, the 'prosecution' of war. He had held Conscientious Objections since he first knew Christ his Saviour, in August 1907. He was given six months' exemption.

The Clerk to the Association of Urban District Councils, wrote to all the Urban Councils in the Country, having prepared a list of occupations which constituted work of national importance that an applicant exempted from military service on the grounds of conscience could perform. These included the sanitary services of local authorities, fire brigade. civil hospitals and asylums. The letter posed two questions: would Bognor Council be willing to engage men having a Conscientious Objection, provided they were suitable? – and what number of vacancies within each department of the Council did they desire to fill?

Bognor Council's reply was short and to the point: 'that they would not employ Conscientious Objectors at any price'.

Civil Volunteers

> 'Seventeen months of war leaves our enemy undefeated and if victory is to be assured every man in 1916 must be prepared to play his part. The more trained men there are in this country, the more secure we are from invasion and the more men who can

> be spared to go abroad then earlier will our enemies be defeated. The more trained troops to be sent abroad, the more important it is for the residue of the male population to be trained, the trenching work done by Volunteers for national defence show that they can vie with the Corps of Engineers.'

Since the decision made early in the war to integrate the Bognor Civil Guard into the Special Constables, volunteer groups had sprung up throughout the country, well organized and very useful to the cause and so popular amongst those ineligible to serve that their existence and contributions were hard to ignore. Consequently, in March 1916 the Government, using the Volunteer Act of 1863, officially recognized the many Volunteers as 'soldiers', not civilians and formed Volunteer Battalions. The Volunteers had been formed in a somewhat haphazard fashion, consisting of men over military age or unable to serve due to employment or health reasons. They provided their own uniforms and equipment at their own expense. Gradually they became recognized as a useful part of home defence and several 'splinter' groups developed, such as the 1st Reserve Motor-Cyclists Brigade, which had been formed to operate in Sussex and was open to any motorist who had a car or motor bike, but restricted to those 'ineligible to enlist for the regular services or who have a genuine reason for not doing so'. Members had to pay an entrance fee of 2s 6d and received a uniform consisting of a three-quarter waterproof overall, khaki breeches, puttees, cap belt and necessary badges. The Brigade was split into three sections - despatch riding, first aid and transport, with drills being held all over Sussex. Various rifle ranges were also put at the Brigade's disposal. Other units were involved in different work:

> 'The course now adopted by the Government will be welcomed by some hundreds of thousands of men of non military age throughout the Country, who have cheerfully and patriotically been sacrificing their leisure hours and a good deal of money in the cause of home defence, guarding bridges, munitions works and taking part in manoeuvres with the regulars. It is feared that it will not be possible at the outset to equip the force with arms and accoutrements, but this will be done as soon as possible.'

The Duke of Norfolk was gazetted to command the Sussex Regiment; locally, Colonel Fryer was placed in charge of 'D' Company which was being raised in Bognor. He announced that he hoped to raise a Company of 150 men to 'defend the town in case of invasion', adding that 'before a man can get interested in military work there would be some monotonous but essential drill to complete'.

The Volunteers held their first official drill on Sunday 13 November 1916, when 'a muster of about eighty recruits being drilled by a Sergeant of the Hampshire Regiment and several ex-Army men'.

A call for more men over military age (between 45 and 60 years) was made to join the Sussex Volunteer Regiment; 'men over military age should not consider themselves precluded from joining the Regiment. Colonel Fryer desires these men should come forward as soon as possible and enrol as drills are being proceeded with and the men already enrolled are becoming efficient.'

The Littlehampton Company and the Arundel Volunteers, complete with their Fife and Drum Band, took part in a march throughout the area with the new Bognor Company 'to excite interest'. Soon Colonel Fryer had over a hundred men on his books.

> 'The Bognor Volunteers are now in full swing and the members are most enthusiastic, meeting Monday and Wednesday evenings from 7pm to 9pm and Sunday afternoons from 3pm to 5pm.'

With the Volunteers having to raise finance for their uniforms and equipment, a fundraising night was held on the Pier. The evening consisted of 'some first rate films' plus 'variety' provided by Mr Arthur Mant, 'the Sussex Yokel' and 'humorous sketches', courtesy of Sergeant Major Millet. Topping the bill was Narenta, 'a speciality dancer' - after which a collection was made.

Those exempted by the local Military Tribunals were also urged to 'show their patriotism by coming forward at once and enrol as members of the Volunteer Corps', sixty of whose members took part in a route march to Barnham on Boxing Day 1916 under Captain J Jubb, who was also the Clerk of the Bognor Urban Council. They were met at North Bersted by Colonel Fryer, who congratulated the men on their appearance.

Lighting Restrictions

The Lighting Restriction offenders were still filling up the local courts:

> 'A good deal of time was again occupied by the Chichester Magistrates at the Petty Sessions on Saturday, hearing more lighting cases from Bognor.'

William Thomas Pepper, of Nyewood Lane, Bognor, was summoned for not effectively shading or obscuring a window 'so that no bright light was shed outside' on 27 December 1915 at 8.30pm. He pleaded not guilty.

Special Officer Treagus said he was with Inspector Rule when he saw a very bright light coming from a house in Nyewood Lane. On going to the house he found it was coming from an incandescent gas light through an upstairs window, the blind of which was not properly drawn, leaving a space about a foot at the top and two feet at the bottom. The beam of light was thrown between thirty and forty feet. The defendant said he was 'very sorry' but his little girl went upstairs and forgot to draw the curtains. He could not dispute it. In his defence Mr Staffurth said the little girl had just come home from school and had neglected to draw the curtains. There was no necessity for the blind because there were curtains. William Pepper was fined ten shillings.

In another case, Muriel Villers, the wife of a serving officer who had been recently mentioned in despatches, was summoned. Special Constable Treagus said he was at the back of the defendant's home, the White House in Belmont Street, when he saw a light showing at 7.40pm on 17 December 1915. It was an electric light showing through the kitchen window, the top part of which had no curtains drawn. It lighted up the building opposite which was about fifteen feet away. He saw Mrs Villiers and asked her to see the light for herself, which she did. She said she was very sorry it happened as they never make a mistake there. The cook switched on the light and forgot to draw the curtains. She said she didn't want the cook summoned as she was only a small girl and would take full responsibility as the householder. Mrs Villiers was fined ten shillings.

A blind gentleman, who lost his sight in the South African War, was the next defendant. Randolph Herbert Turner, of Sunny Cottage, Tennyson Road, Bognor, was led into court by a young lady.

Special Officer Treagus said he was with Inspector Rule when they saw a very bright light coming from the back of Sunny Cottage and on going to the house he saw it was caused by an incandescent light showing from a large sitting room window, the curtains of which were not properly drawn, leaving two spaces, one of about six inches and the other of about eight inches. A beam of light was thrown about sixty yards, lighting up a house on the opposite side of Nelson Road. After long arguments the case was dismissed, the Magistrate commenting, 'you have summoned a man who would give anything to be able to see a bright light'.

Cases of this nature continued to be heard throughout the year.

Bognor War Hospital

After negotiations between the War Office and the Bognor Town Council, plans were laid to build a war hospital in Victoria Drive. Initially, this was to hold 400 beds, quickly expanding to over 2000. The hospital would consist of hutments and cover a wide area. Hospital members of the Army Sanitary Council paid several visits to the town, inspecting the site and expressing their approval of the bracing seaside air which would aid recovery. After their last visit in April 1916 everything seemed set and ready to go. However, a week or two later the whole scheme was cancelled and despite the best efforts of the Town Council to receive a formal notification letter as to the reason, all they received was a letter from Brigadier General Baker Brown in which he wrote:

> 'I am sorry, although I feel sure that the facilities of fine air, a good beach and the general comfort the town affords would a have been of benefit to our wounded soldiers, the scheme will not go ahead.'

Bognor's Worst Month of the War

June 1916 brought more bad news than any other during the war. Two main events were responsible, the Battle of Jutland and a diversionary action by the Royal Sussex Regiment at on the eve of the Somme.

It had long been predicted that a major sea battle between the Royal Navy's Grand Fleet and the German High Seas Fleet was inevitable and on the night on 31 May and 1 June the two met at the Battle of Jutland. Many local men, both reservists and regulars, were serving in the Royal Navy and fought in that battle, the details of which need not be described here.

> 'It is impossible to state at all accurately the number of local casualties which will have to be recorded as the result of the great Naval Battle in the North Sea', wrote the *Bognor Observer*, but it is certain that this corner of West Sussex has contributed heavily to the list of brave men who lost their lives in the greatest sea fight of modern times. Bognor has lost brave sons, brothers, fathers, husbands, who will be seen no more.'

Eleven local sailors were killed in action that night as the battle raged in the North Sea. Five days later another local sailor lost his life when his ship, carrying Lord Kitchener to Russia was mined off the north of Scotland. At the end of the month more bad news arrived.

The men of the Southdowns Battalions of the Royal Sussex Regiment, who volunteered throughout Sussex in the early days of the war, having completed their training, were moved to the Front in March 1916. With the Somme Offensive planned for 1 July the Southdowns were selected to take part in a 'diversionary action' to the north of the

HMS Black Prince*, lost with all hands at Jutland, including five Bognor sailors.*

main attack on 30 June. This was to be the first time that they had gone 'over the top' and all three battalions were to take part. The plan went horribly wrong, with a large loss of life, so much so the day has since been called the 'Day that Sussex Died'. The *Bognor Observer* wrote:

> 'In accordance with expectations, the casualty lists during the past few days have been very heavy and the prominent part which the Royal Sussex took in the great 'push' is reflected in the large number of killed or wounded.'

Writing home from a London hospital to which he was evacuated to recover from his wounds a few days later, Sergeant JJ Isted of Bognor wrote:

> 'We were making an attack at dawn, but we never took the German trenches, as they were waiting for us and mowed us down as fast as we got there. We lost a lot of men, including I believe a good many killed and wounded from Bognor.'

Thirteen local men died that morning, with many others wounded. The Battle of the Somme commenced the following day, lasting until the onset of winter, during which another forty six Bognorians were killed.

The Pier Theatre

A series of official films of the Somme were put on general release and shown locally at the Pier Theatre:

> 'The Battle of the Somme film is a masterpiece which has created so much discussion wherever it has been shown, the sense of introducing the huge guns of modern warfare are a revelation to the uninitiated.'

This was followed a few weeks later with another film depicting the Battle of Ancre:

> 'All Bognor should go and see the official war film depicting the Battle of Ancre and the advance of the tanks. This is one of the most remarkable subjects that has ever been filmed and has

Bognor Pier, where many hundreds watched the film of the Somme.

the additional recommendation that there is no 'fake' in it. Those who remember the Battle of the Somme films should not fail to see this, which is even more attractive than that series. Such films as these bring the war home to one very vividly and it almost amounts to a duty to see them. The tanks at the Pier are the biggest draw the popular theatre has had for many a day. The Somme picture was thought to be wonderful, but this is even more wonderful.'

The showing of these films in the Pier Theatre did indeed prove popular, as did a follow up, war pictures shown as a magic lantern show:

'A three day programme of the war in pictures and stories, show in vivid scenes of what is really happening in the great European conflict, personally narrated by that well known and intrepid war correspondent, Dr Howard, who has just returned from the fighting area after many thrilling adventures, who will personally narrate the many exciting incidents and fully explain the scenes as they are shown on the screen at each performance.

> One performance a day only at 3pm and the seats cost from 3d to a shilling.'

On the surface life continued normally, the 1916 'season' being very successful, with military bands playing on the Pier and both bandstands, although some residents complained in the press that being 'Reserve Bands' the musical standard was below that of pre war days. This incensed Private Eddie Stares, a butcher from London Road, Bognor, when he read this in the *Bognor Observer* which had been sent to him at the Front. He 'invited' those who were complaining to come to the Front and hear the real 'military music of shot and shell'.

The Olympian Gardens and Kursaal were all busy as the press reported that 30,000 people were in town for the August Bank Holiday, despite the war.

The Prime Minister's Visit

One special visitor to Aldwick was the Prime Minister, Mr Asquith:

> 'The Prime Minister is staying at Aldwick for some weeks, going up and down to London as the occasion requires. During his stay he has had the opportunity of seeing British airships on the coast.'

He may have also experienced the air raid measures which were again put to the test when a Zeppelin flew over Bognor: 'a warm reception was accorded and when the guns spoke, it climbed to a higher, safer level'.

Mr Asquith stayed in Bognor for a couple of weeks, celebrating his 68th birthday here before returning to London.

CHAPTER 6

1917

War Front

In 1917 in the Middle East, three battles at Gaza against the Turks, which commenced in March and ended in November, accounted for many local casualties. Deaths also occurred after the battles as British prisoners of war suffered appallingly at the hands of the Turks, Corporal Albert Powell and Gunner Richard Powell, both of South Bersted, dying in captivity.

In Europe the Battle of Arras in April and May was followed by Messines Ridge in June. The Third Battle of Ypres (popularly known as Passchendaele) fought from July until November and two Battles at Cambrai also accounted for many deaths as the Allies strove to break through the German defences. Sixty-six local men lost their lives in 1917.

At the beginning of 1917, His Majesty King George V made a 'dignified and inspiring statement', informing the people in a straightforward way of the seriousness of the situation:

> 'Young England has responded nobly in these stirring times, but it is not sufficient. Thousands who were unaffected by the call of the trumpet are confronted with a question that demands an answer. Thousands have welcomed with a great thankfulness the opportunity to take a more active share in the struggle than circumstance before permitted and splendid Battalions of Volunteers up and down the Country have come forward. But there are those who have not yet come forward and answered

the call. Will they wait until it is too late? Or will they step forward to the place that is vacant and that no one else can fill, so that in the days to come they will know, though no one asks them, what did they do in the war? They did their duty.'

Local Hero

Corporal W Powell, of Manor Cottages, Felpham, the son of Mr and Mrs John Powell, served with a Heavy Battery, Royal Field Artillery. Writing from France to his parents in April 1917, he informed them of his proud news:

'I have some good news to tell you. I have received the Military Medal, I won it yesterday and I have had a day of hand shaking with the Officers and chums of our battery. My arm is ready to drop off so you must excuse this scribble. Of course I haven't received the medal yet, I get the ribbon now and when I come home after the war the medal will no doubt be presented to me. My Officer Commanding presented me with the ribbon. I won the medal for bravery in the field, that is for sticking to my gun under heavy fire. I think I am the first lad from Felpham to get the Military Medal so of course I feel very proud.'

Food Shortages

In February 1917 Germany declared unrestricted submarine war against ships supplying the United Kingdom with food and essentials. It was not long before food shortages were causing a problem and, with the Government introducing food price controls, a local Food Control Committee was set up with considerable powers. Sugar was one example; anyone ordering large amounts for jam making had their gardens and allotments inspected by the Committee members to see if they contained enough fruit trees or bushes to justify their purchases.

'Though not yet desperate, the food situation is far from reassuring and in view of the apparent determination of some people not to save it, they will not be surprised if food regulations of a drastic character are shortly framed.

'At Bognor the situation is not alarming, though there is a scarcity in one or two commodities, notably sugar. We

> understand that the authorities do not suspect hoarding, but waste is causing much thought and the dustmen have been asked to report any apparent abnormal waste of food. It is the intention of the Food Committee to visit offenders and emphasise the importance of economy. It is also suggested that each household should be placed on a particular panel, so that bakers may be rationed in flour.'

Cards were then delivered throughout the town asking householders to co-operate with them in reducing their consumption of food and to encourage the use of substitutes for bread, flour and potatoes:

> 'I am instructed to write and ask you personally to assist in the campaign by adopting in your family the National Scheme of Voluntary Rations and inducing others you may meet to do the same. If you are prepared to do so, show a pledge card to this effect in your window. The official pledge card, in red, white and blue, will be supplied to you for this purpose. At the moment the shortage of bread is the predominant problem and the immediate reduction by at least 20% must be effected.'

Townsfolk were also urged not to purchase more foodstuffs than necessary for immediate use, so as not to inflate prices, and were also asked to notify of any suspected profiteering. Bakers came in for particular criticism, as the price of bread had risen to four pence three farthings a loaf, leading to accusations that bakers were in fact on the make. This so incensed some soldiers that they wrote to the *Bognor Observer*:

> 'Some of us, when we were called up, rather than go over the water and fight the common enemy, would I fancy prefer to engage in battle with the bakers who seem to be feathering their nests at the expense of our wives and children.'

However, the bakers considered the price of bread to reflect the costs of making it. Added to their problems were the fact that many bakers had been called up.

At that time the Bognor Tribunal called another baker to review his situation regarding military service. The Baker's Association made it clear that 'they did not see how they could release any more men, it was impossible to obtain men in their places. There would be a shortage of bread in the town if any more were taken.' The message seemed to be getting through. The baker, a married man, aged 35, was given a six month exemption.

The price of milk had also risen to 7d a quart and 1d extra for sealed bottles. Many local dairymen delivered milk in the area and it was felt that some were 'taking advantage' and increasing their prices. The Ministry of Food then set the price of a quart to be 'ladled out' for 6d.

A deputation of the Dairymen's Association met with the Food Control Committee to explain why the retail price of milk had been raised to 7d. The Committee 'received their deputation of Messrs Heaver, Money and others, but heard no reason expressed by the deputation to alter their opinion that the maximum price that milk should be sold in Bognor should be 6d a quart'.

The deputation then stated that they would put their case to the Food Controller, whilst in the meantime acknowledging that they had to honour the lower prices. Their appeal, however, failed.

In order to back up their request for food saving, a campaign of lectures and demonstrations 'for teaching in a practical manner how to provide suitable substitutes' was organised. These were advertised in the local press and 'those desirous of assisting in this campaign should make a point of attending these lectures, where ladies will be in attendance to supply recipes and give advice'.

One lecture on wartime cookery in May 1917 proved to be very popular:

> 'The initiation of Bognor's wartime cookery lectures must have surprised even some of the promoters by its success. Armed with notebooks and pencils the housewives of the town attended Miss Ainslie's opening lecture in the Lyon Street school last week in such numbers that the accommodation proved to be quite inadequate.'

A lecture also took place at the Pier Theatre, complete with lantern slides, encouraging people to grow more vegetables, particularly potatoes, which attracted an 'appreciative audience'.

Municipal Piggeries

To supplement the food supply Bognor Council announced in February 1917 the purchase of pigs to be kept in purpose built Municipal Piggeries controlled by the Local Government Board. The site of the refuse destructor was chosen for the pigs' home. This would ensure that there was a ready supply of food for them as 'a lot of food waste had been going on there for many years past.'

Bognor's leading light in this project was Oswald Bridges, the Borough Surveyor, who wrote a series of articles which were not only printed in *'The Surveyor'* magazine, but were reprinted in the American publication *'Engineering News Record'*, to 'show Americans what British Urban Councils are doing to meet the shortage in animal food in England and to act as an incentive to the people in the United States'.

> 'Bognor is literally going the whole hog in food production and is embarking on the wilder sensations which fall to the lot of the pig dealer in these days. The Council have decided to undertake the keeping of pigs at the Council Refuse Depot and that twelve sties are to be constructed at an estimated cost of £50 for the housing of such pigs. A number of pigs are to be purchased at a cost of £60, the number and kind of pigs to be determined later. Pig keeping is a specialist subject and it is doubtful that any member of the Council possessed that knowledge so special sources of wisdom would be consulted before the Council begin operations.'

The piggery was well constructed to house up to sixty inmates, commencing with the purchase of three sows and were looked after by the Council staff on the site. Almost immediately the pigs became 'town favourites', their diet of waste food collected by the dustmen being supplemented by 'scraps provided by the public'. Cinema goers were asked to provide scraps for them via a picture on the screen and postcards of the pigs were said to be 'selling like hot cakes'. Public interest increased when seven little piglets were born, bringing the total to nineteen and their fame began to spread:

> 'Bognor's pioneer municipal pigs are gradually spreading their fame. Among the latest visitors to their salubrious site has been

Lady Amherst of Hackney, the Director of the National Salvage Council (Rural Section). She said a number of nice things about piggy and his progress:

'Bognor has created quite a record in this department and is being held up as an example of what can be done in food production, for other towns to copy and I hope that the efforts made will not be relaxed until all danger of a shortage in our food supply had been relaxed.'

The pigs, however, were kept to supplement the local food chain and make a profit for the Council:

'The Bognor pigs still keep their tails well up notwithstanding the prevalent depression in the world of pork. The Council Accountants show a profit of £330 for the town piggery to date and now a good start has been made a further profit of £150 to £200 is anticipated. Surveyors from all parts of the country it seems have been to Bognor to see the pigs.'

Despite their popularity, in a letter to the *Bognor Observer,* Oswald Bridges wrote:

'They are not there as ornaments, but for the food of man and they must be made to pay and show a good profit. This can easily be done by each householder helping to feed their own and the ratepayers pigs by saving the scraps.'

The example by the Bognor Council set off a pig keeping boom in the town, with pigs being kept by private individuals on spare or waste ground. There were so many of them that the Area Live Stock Commissioner issued an order 'that pigs may be slaughtered by any person, provided that in all cases the carcase is sent to an authorised Government slaughter house. Any pig owner wishing to follow this course would have to obtain written consent. This system will appeal to a fair number of pig owners, who not only having the meat to eat would be paid 2s 6d for the carcase if it was 'in good condition'.

An Overcharging Butcher

The prices butchers were charging for meat were also fixed and reviewed monthly. The Committee received a complaint that one butcher in the town was charging more than the fixed prices. He was summoned to answer a charge that he had sold 'a shoulder of mutton weighing four and three quarter pounds at 2s 2d per lb, as against 1s 4 halfpenny a lb, as per the Committee's current schedule. He was also charged with selling a neck of home killed mutton on the same date for 1s 6d per lb, being 4d halfpenny per lb in excess of the fixed maximum price. He was told that 'legal action' would follow and was subsequently fined £25 plus costs on each of the two charges. 'A flagrant example of overcharging', commented the Bench.

Bleak Bognor

In the summer of 1917 an appeal to Bognor's population was issued regarding their use of Doctors:

> 'The Army needs all the Doctors of military age who can be spared and Bognor has answered the appeal to the best of its ability. This means that the Doctors who are left must work much harder than usual and they can only give the medical service that is really necessary. If the public can help them this can be done in many ways, with a little forethought. Be loyal to your Doctor if he is on service, tell another Doctor you may go to while he is away, that your own is on service. You will then be attended to and when he comes back, both you and your Doctor who has been acting for him will have the satisfaction of knowing that you did your duty by him, while he was doing his duty by the Country.'

Price controls were also introduced for coal in 1917 following recent pay rises to miners, many of whom were soldiers recalled to the mines to maintain supplies to the war machine. House coal prices were fixed at 38 shillings per ton for 'best kitchen coal', whilst 'best house coal' fetched £2 per ton. As the 1917-18 winter approached it was estimated that Bognor would need 6500 tons of coal between October and April for domestic use, although it was thought unlikely that amount would be delivered because Bognor was 'so far away from the coal producing area'. A rationing plan was therefore drawn up which impressed on the people the need for economy. For the winter all houses of less than four rooms were allocated 2 cwt per week, five and six roomed houses would get 3 cwt. Larger houses containing seven to ten rooms received 1 ton per month, eleven and twelve rooms were issued with 1 ton 7cwt per month, whilst those with between thirteen and fifteen rooms would receive 2 tons per month. Houses larger than that had 2 tons 10 cwt irrespective of their size.

Further hardships for the population were announced by the Bognor Gas Company, who drew their attention to a new order made under the Defence of the Realm Act 'whereby it becomes compulsory for the users of gas and electricity to reduce their consumptions of these commodities by one sixth per three months'. The reason behind this order was explained by the Board of Trade, if usage was not reduced they would find themselves 'totally unable to maintain an adequate supply throughout the District'. A lot of their problems stemmed from 'depleted staff' as the war continued to need more manpower. The Bognor Gas Company also requested that, due to the uncertain disturbed conditions of the coal market, the Council should economise as much as possible on street lighting. A further restriction concerned the local shops, which commenced 6pm closing on Mondays, Tuesdays and Thursdays, remaining at 7.30pm on Fridays and Saturdays. Chemists, hairdressers and tobacconists were exempted from this order. The public were told 'it is a patriotic duty to shop early and so save light'.

Without a doubt, 1917 was a bleak year in Bognor. The war had been raging for three years and five months with little sign of ending. The casualty lists of the town had continued to rise, both in fatalities and injuries. Food and fuel were in short supply and there was no sign that in 1918 the situation would improve.

CHAPTER 7

1918

War Front

By the spring of 1918 Russia had signed the Treaty of Brest Litovsk, thus allowing the Germans to move over a million men and some three thousand guns to the west where the British and French, exhausted and depleted after the battles of 1917, strove to contain them. The German aim was to end the war by separating the British and French armies before the Americans arrived in significant numbers on the Western Front. At that time they were being escorted across the Atlantic in large numbers by the Royal Navy. The German offensive commenced on 21 March and continued for the next five months, before the Allies halted it and then went on the offensive themselves in August near Amiens. The third Battle of the Somme was fought in late August and early September, followed by a break through at Ypres in late September and early October. Fighting continued until November, Sergeant Charles Bliss of Bognor was amongst the last local casualties when he was killed at the Battle of the Sambre Canal on 4 November. Sergeant Bliss was awarded the Military Medal for his actions on that day. On 11 November 1918 the Armistice was signed but not before a further seventy-two local men had lost their lives.

Local Hero

In August 1918 the *Bognor Observer* reported the following:

> 'We are pleased to hear that a former smart young forward in the Bognor football eleven has secured the distinction of a

Military Medal in France. The name of Pinchard in this connexion is familiar to many of our readers and it is as Corporal William Frank Pinchard of the Royal Garrison Artillery that he has achieved honour in his Country's cause. The son of Mr and Mrs Pinchard of Walton Cottage, Walton Road, joined the army seven years ago and after serving in Hong Kong went to France three years ago. In a recent letter to his parents he says:

'You asked about the medal. Well we only get the ribbon out here and the medal at home. I don't think I shall be the same as a good many of you speak of, but I shall get through. I don't think I ever had such a gruelling as we had on the retreat, I did not lie down for eight days and only got sleep on the tenth. I had a rope in my hand and cut it through and I never got touched and then I had to keep on firing.'

Recruitment

Manpower was still needed and an appeal was made for older men to enlist:

Not too old at fifty.

> 'Fit men over military age and up to fifty years of age are urgently wanted for the Army, principally for home service and special conditions are being offered. Men who are not liable under the Military Service Acts, but enlist voluntarily in the Royal Garrison Artillery or the Army Service Corps (Motor Transport), will be guaranteed service at home and as near to their homes as it is possible to place them. They will not be transferred to any other branch of the service without their written consent. There are vacancies, too, for older men in the Royal Air Force and the Royal Engineers (Inland Water Transport). These men will be liable for service at home or abroad, but there are very interesting occupations open to them in our latest fighting arm. Any recruiting official will gladly give information to prospective recruits from civil life, or to discharged non-commissioned officers and men, who though under no obligation, are prepared to enlist voluntarily in response to the present call.'

By the end of the war the total number of local men with the Colours well exceeded 1000.

Food Shortages

As the war lingered into its fifth year the food shortages became an increasing problem; 'food economy is the urgent necessity of the day', headlined the local paper, which also warned that if not done voluntarily then 'food rationing' would be introduced. A public meeting addressed by a Captain More 'who advised on such things' was held at the Queens Hall, Canada Grove, 'to awaken the people of Bognor to this need', as if they needed to be told:

> 'To avoid an egg famine, chickens could be fed on household refuse and meal, they can live without corn, anybody with a piece of waste ground could keep a flock and discharged soldiers could be employed looking after them. Rabbits could be farmed; peasants in Normandy lived on rabbits all the time. If you use waste food, rabbits could be fed for 4d per lb.'

He also encouraged people to grow more vegetables, keep fowls, pigs and turkeys for the cultivation of food and urged people to take advantage of the extra hour's daylight now that the Daylight Saving Bill had recently been passed by Parliament. The Council wanted to take over Mr Wingate's field in Hawthorn Road for new allotments, but this would have affected his dairy business as he would have had to sell his cows and the town would go short of milk. Unused building plots were then made available for allotments:

POTATOES in 1918.

Last year the County of Sussex

Produced 26,600 Tons of Potatoes.

Consumed 58,900 Tons of Potatoes.

Deficit 32,300 Tons.

LORD RHONDDA and Mr. PROTHERO appeal to every man who has a farm, a garden, or an allotment to PLANT MORE POTATOES and make the County

SELF-SUPPORTING.

> 'It is evident that the increase in the cost of food is becoming a serious matter and it behoves every patriotic person to assist as far as possible in maintaining the food supply. Applications are urgently required as the time is rapidly approaching when seeds for potatoes etc. must be planted if a crop is to be obtained this season.'

Upwards of fifty persons other than regular allotment holders took advantage of this scheme, the whole of the area being utilized with potatoes as the main crop. In support of the campaign, a lecture on how to grow potatoes was held at the Pier Theatre:

> 'A good number of interested persons derived much benefit from a capital lecturer, lantern slides were used to illustrate his remarks and the Council are to be congratulated on their enterprise in securing the services of such an authority on vegetable production.'

By now, women were being recruited to replace conscripted men to drive motor tractors on the land, 'those enlisting will have a month's training, wages will be 25 shillings a week rising to £2 10 shillings when efficient'. In order to encourage them, a film was shown at the Pier Theatre highlighting the splendid work women have done on the land, whilst a speaker explained the terms of employment and urged them to join, 'as the Army cannot release any soldiers this year for agricultural work it is imperative for women to volunteer to supply the deficiency'.

Meanwhile, the volunteer war work continued apace and requests from the Front for various articles still arrived. One was via the Vicar of South Bersted, who was stationed in Italy as a Chaplain to the Forces. He wrote in February, upon receiving what he requested:

> 'Yesterday two cases containing four 'Decca' gramophones were delivered to me. I wish I could put into words my joy when I saw the cases opened and the splendid Deccas which were in perfect condition. In each of our hospital buildings we now have a gramophone and so the bed patients will be able to get some music.'

Fishing

To help provide more food a scheme to speed up the supply of fish was devised by the Bognor Urban District Clerk, Mr Joseph Jubb. War Fishing Permits only allowed amateurs to go to sea with professional fishermen. He introduced amateur permits so they could go on their own and take a novice volunteer. An Angling Brigade was formed: Class A, Fulltime; Class B, Weekenders; and Class C, Occasional. The scheme was successful; twenty one Bognor amateur fishing permit holders landed nearly one ton of fish during its first month compared with one and a half tons for the whole of the previous year's season.

The Welcome Club

Since the beginning of the war, the Women's Institute had operated a Welcome Club in Waterloo Square for serving soldiers and sailors home on leave. In June 1918 a Sunday Welcome Club was also opened, following a concert to raise enough funds and was soon attracting large numbers of servicemen. In November 1918 the two were combined.

> 'On Thursday afternoon the first of a series of parties for wounded soldiers took place at the Bognor Women's Institute. Forty wounded soldiers were invited, through the kindness of some members, and were entertained to tea at which no signs of rationing were visible. On Sunday the Institute was opened to any member of HM Forces and tea was provided at a very small

cost. A large number of soldiers availed themselves of the opportunity, especially at tea time.'

The Club was always busy:

'The number of soldiers who take advantage of this institution, which is open every Sunday afternoon and evening, increases weekly. The club provides refreshments at cost price to all soldiers and sailors who desire to take advantage of the opportunity of having a good tea at a moderate cost. Letters can also be written there, while a piano is provided for their entertainment.'

Another good idea emerged from the Club:

'The Soldiers Welcome Club appeal for presents of eggs, lettuce, fruit etc., to be handed in on Sundays as it is proposed to open a market on Mondays and Thursdays commencing on 4 July for the sale of vegetables and fruit produced from all allotment holders who can send them. The produce must be of a proper marketable quality and will be received from 7am to 8.30am and paid for in cash at Covent Garden prices. The trade will have the preference of purchasing the same from 8am to 8.30am and the general public from that time to 10am cash only. It is hoped that all allotment holders will avail themselves of this new scheme of disposing of their surplus, which will prevent waste, at the same time enriching their pockets and also be a means of enabling the general public to secure fresh and hopefully cheaper vegetables.'

Home Front

The 1918 season opened and visitors were delighted on the Monday of the opening of the Military Band Season, performances being given daily in the morning and evening at the Western Bandstand and in the afternoon in the Eastern Bandstand.

'The Band opening the first fortnight is that of the 3rd Reserve Cavalry. If wet, performances will be given in the Queens Hall.'

The season of Band Concerts went so well that the Council extended it by a further fortnight into September, at the Western Bandstand only. The use of the Eastern Bandstand had to be curtailed because of a lack of manpower to move the chairs from one to the other!

Influenza Pandemic

A serious global influenza epidemic swept the country in 1918, causing great concern among the population. In Bognor the Sanitary Committee, in conjunction with the West Sussex Medical Officer, issued a number of posters setting out precautionary hints regarding the disease and how to prevent infection. Other restrictions were also announced. The Pier Company was instructed to prohibit the admission of children under the age of sixteen to any of their performances at their cinema theatre and to allow an interval between performances of at least forty five minutes. The theatre had also to be disinfected and thoroughly ventilated on a daily basis.

Sadly, the epidemic claimed victims in Bognor, including soldiers on leave who had avoided the dangers of the battlefield only to fall victim of influenza.

This was the final piece of bad news for Bognor, as in November the war ended and the Armistice was signed.

ARMISTICE DAY
VICTORY

Glorious and Complete

The Armistice was signed at five o'clock this morning

Hostilities ceased on all fronts at 11 o'clock today

Bognor Beaming

'It is a mystery from where all the flags and bunting came with which Bognor was decorated on Monday. As soon as the news came through, Bognor was decorated with the flags of all our Allies and a brave show they made, lighting up a dull November day in a most effective manner. The people appeared as it were from nowhere and in a short time the streets were filled with jubilant people unashamed of their joy at the great tidings. The scene can best be likened to a busy Christmas Eve, but in one respect it was different, very few purchases were made, although a brisk trade was done in flags, bunting and trumpets. Some of the shops closed in the dinner hour and others earlier than usual.

The children fully appreciated the glad tidings and there was scarcely a child to be seen without their red, white and blue. Perambulators and bicycles were gaily decorated. In the evening the youngsters appeared with fireworks, which they let off with great glee, having been prohibited from doing so for so long.

A large number of people were out in the evening rejoicing in the lighting of the lamps and the relief from the lighting regulations. One did not realise how the lamps were missed, until they were put on again.

A Thanksgiving Service will be held at St John's Church on Wednesday afternoon at 3pm.'

The service was heartily responded to by the citizens, it was quite impossible for more people to have been present. Two hundred more seats had been placed in the church but in spite of this the aisle, chancel, organ loft and vestry were all crowded and hundreds were unable to get inside. In view of this, a service was also held outside. The collection, amounting to £40 4s 4d was for the Bognor Red Cross Society and created a record in Bognor for a single service.

Amidst all the celebrations there was also much sorrow and despair. How the widows, children and parents of those who had made the supreme sacrifice must have felt over the next few months, as the surviving servicemen returned, or how their children in the playgrounds coped, listening to their friends' joy of having 'Daddy' back home, only they could known. Many homes had suffered multiple losses, with brothers, fathers and sons having lost their lives.

CHAPTER 8

From Wives to Widows

Throughout the war, the early morning knock on the door heralding the arrival of the postman was met each day with trepidation in hundreds of Bognor homes. Hopefully, the post would contain a letter from a loved one reassuring his family that all was well, with possible news about some home leave in the near future. These letters would be read many times, as they were the only communication between the horrors of the Front and the home fireside and were greatly treasured.

However, the post could also bring news of the worst kind and everyone dreaded seeing the small buff OHMS envelope on the doormat. One can imagine the scene as a wife or parent picked up the envelope and, with hands shaking, opened it to read the enclosure. It could contain one of three forms, depending on the circumstances. One would advise the relatives that their loved one had been seriously wounded and was in hospital. An anxious wait could then occur before any more news was received. Further letters would sometimes arrive from nursing sisters and hospital chaplains giving progress reports, if the injuries were such that the victims were unable to write.

Perhaps the worst torment for the anxious relatives was the enclosure informing them that their loved one had been reported as 'missing'. It was sometimes many months before their fate was known. Often the International Red Cross was approached for help in finding out what had happened to the men. In more than one local case they were successful in tracing those who had, for instance, become Prisoners of War. Usually the first that the families knew of their plight was the arrival of a plain postcard, informing them that their loved one was a PoW and whereabouts in Germany they were being held: at least now they knew they were alive. After the first contact, letters could be exchanged and parcels of necessary items sent via the good offices of the Red Cross. Others had to wait until another buff OHMS envelope arrived, informing them that their man was still 'missing' but now 'presumed killed'.

The third and most dreaded enclosure simply stated that 'It is my painful duty to inform you that a report has been received from the War Office notifying the death of.......'.

Occasionally the news was transmitted by telegram. The sight of the telegram boy in his uniform and pill box hat cycling down the road was a heart stopping moment for many people as they anxiously waited to see the house at which he would call. Once the news had been received, relatives and neighbours rallied around the distraught family, fully aware that theirs could be the next notification. Essex Road, Bognor, particularly suffered, with nearly half the homes affected by injuries and deaths.

After the official notification of a death had been received a personal letter from one of the victim's officers usually arrived. These tended to be formulaic, designed perhaps to soften the impact, but often containing graphic details of the 'awful event' and the whereabouts of their loved one's grave. Comrades would also write on occasions; these were genuine messages of grief in losing a valued 'chum' with whom they had lived and faced death on a daily basis and would possibly contain the victim's last messages home before they succumbed to their wounds.

For the relatives the usual grieving process could not be followed. There would be no closure, no funeral to arrange, no chance to say goodbye; widows, children and parents just had to struggle on with their lives. Below are just a few examples:

Jack Saigeman was a naval reservist working for the gas company. He lived at Ivy Lane, South Bersted, with his new bride, Lily. Called up at the outbreak of war he served on HMS *Good Hope*, which was sunk off Chile, with all hands, in the Battle of Coronel Sea in 1914.

Jack had been married to Lily only a few weeks and shortly after receiving notification of his death she received his last letter, worried because he had not heard from her. This was because of his ship's constant movements and the forces post had not caught up with him.

Jack's ship, HMS Good Hope, *lost with all hands, many being reservists from West Sussex.*

The letter Lily received from Jack arrived at Christmas and contained these poignant words....'I should like very much to get a line from you Lily, the time seems so long to me and I should feel so much better if only I knew that my wife was alright.'

By the time Lily read that she was a widow.

If Mrs Annie Begg, of Lyora, Gordon Avenue, Bognor, had heard the words of the Recruiting Officer at a meeting in Bognor in 1915, when he stated, 'if a soldier is shot at six in the morning, he will be in bed in England at six in the evening', she would, no doubt, have been very angry. Her husband, Robert was shot in the left leg on the morning of 18 November 1916 and lay in the mud on the battlefield for two days and nights before being found.

Robert enlisted in the Royal West Surrey Regiment and was wounded on what proved to be the last day of the Battle of Ancre. He was eventually rescued and taken to the Base Hospital where he died the following day. The Matron wrote to Annie:

> 'I am very grieved to tell you that your dear husband died early this morning. He had an attack of haemorrhage and was taken to the operating theatre and obliged to have his leg amputated, he died some few hours after it. He will be buried with full Military Honours. The cemetery is quite well kept and the graves well looked after. I am indeed sorry for you in this dreadful sorrow and you will be glad to know that we all did our very best for him.
>
> Matron.'

In many instances the widows were left with a young family. Thomas Brockhurst was married to Kate and they lived at Spire View, Chalcroft Lane, North Bersted, with their young children. Tommy enlisted in the Royal Fusiliers in May 1916, leaving his job as the groundsman at the

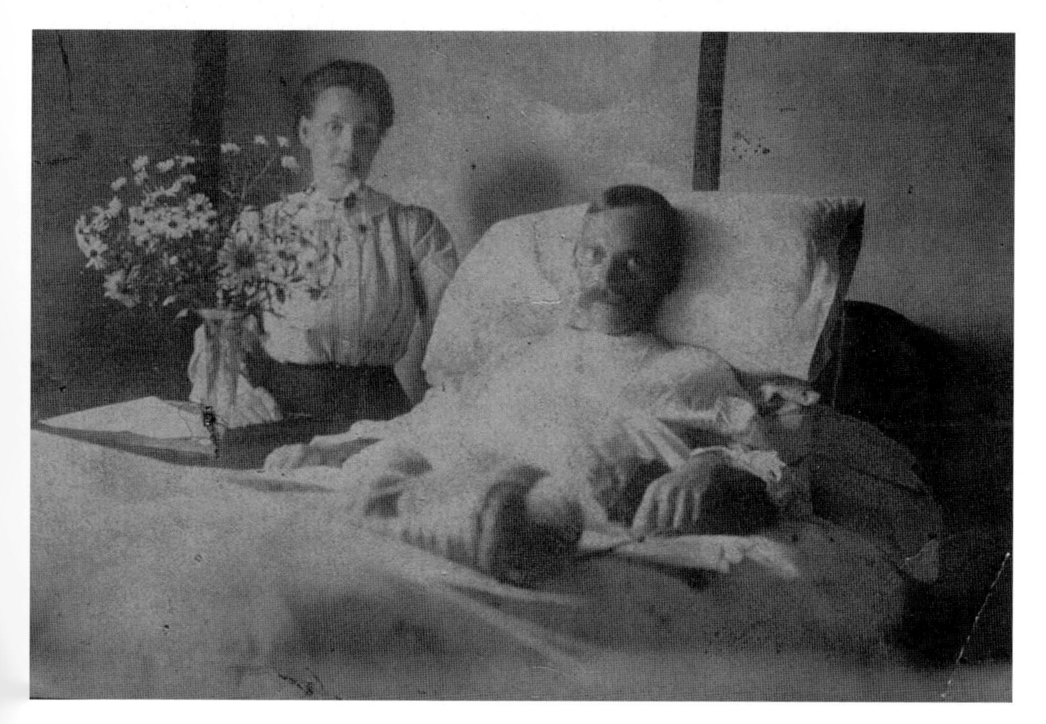

Kate and the children, Florence and John face life alone. (Photographs courtesy of Sandra Morley)

Bognor Croquet Grounds in Victoria Road. On 14 September 1917 he received serious gunshot wounds in his face and also suffered a fractured spine. He was transferred back to Blighty for treatment in No 2 New Zealand General Hospital, where he lay seriously ill until his death on 10 January 1918, aged 31. His funeral took place five days later, when he was buried in the Bognor Cemetery.

In proud and loving memory of my dear husband Private Thomas Brockhurst who died on 10 January 1918 of wounds after four months of suffering, cheerfully and patiently borne.

One Less at Home
The Happy Circle Broken
A Dear Face Missed Day by Day

From His Sorrowing Wife and Children

(At least eighty three Bognor wives became widows because of the war and possibly twice that number of children lost their fathers. Several other ladies 'betrothed' to soldiers lost their future husbands.)

CHAPTER 9

Patriotic Families

Several families were highlighted in the local press for their 'proud record of military service', with many sons all serving:

> Mr and Mrs Holden of Pagham were reported to have had eight sons serving: Alfred (Lost at Sea 1917), Charles, Jesse and Joseph were in the Royal Navy, whilst John, Osman and Albert served with the Royal Engineers and William with the Middlesex Regiment.
>
> Mr and Mrs Denyer of 38 Chapel Street had six family members serving. Mr Denyer, aged 52, was serving with the Royal Defence Corps at Dover and his five sons were also serving: Private F Denyer, aged 24 was discharged injured on three occasions, but still re-enlisted. Corporal H Denyer, aged 23, was serving with the Royal Sussex Regiment in France. Private A Denyer, aged 22, was also in France with the Royal Warwickshire Regiment, and Private W Denyer, was serving with the Royal West Surrey Regiment. Even the youngest son, Trumpeter R Denyer, joined 14th King's Hussars - he was 17 years old.
>
> Another six men - four sons and two sons-in-law of Mrs Stammer, of 4 St Claire Terrace, Linden Road, were also serving: Lieutenant Frank Stammer was with the Royal Garrison Artillery, as was Bombardier Frank Stammer; Christopher and

Oliver Stammer both served with the Royal West Kent Regiment in Persia; Private Richard Johnson, son-in-law, was with 24th County of London Rifles; and Sergeant John Eaton, son in law, was with a Machine Gun Battery.

Six brothers, the sons of Mr and Mrs Littlechild of 3 Victoria Cottages, South Bersted, all enlisted: Privates E (Killed in Action, 1917) and GE Littlechild were both with the Royal Sussex Regiment; Private A Littlechild was with the Royal Army Service Corps; Private SH Littlechild was in a Trench Mortar Battery; whilst Gunners W and F Littlechild (the latter Killed in Action 1915) served with the Royal Field Artillery.

Mr F Wingate, a dairy farmer of Highgate, also had all his sons serving: Alfred was with the Royal Naval Air Service; William, a Sergeant Instructor with the Royal Garrison Artillery, alongside Edmund who was a bombardier; Ernest Wingate was in the Royal Sussex Regiment and was discharged badly wounded; finally, Arthur was serving with the King's Royal Rifles

Mrs Squires of 17 Parrametta Terrace, Ockley Road, had five sons and one son-in-law serving: Private F Squires was with the Hampshire Regiment, whilst all the others were with the Royal Sussex Regiment; Privates H and P W Squires were with the 9th Battalion, Private A J Squires and Private G Farley (Died of Wounds, 1916) were with 12th Battalion.

Many Bognor streets were deprived of their menfolk as more and more volunteered or were conscripted. Chapel Street, Wood Street, Linden Road, Longford Road, Annandale Avenue, Highfield Road, Canada Grove, Argyle Road, Ockley Road, Steyne Street and many others all played their part. Essex Road, however, stood out from the rest for the numbers of men serving, as featured by *The Bognor Observer* in June 1916:

'This Bognor thoroughfare has done splendidly in giving its manhood to the Colours. Out of sixty homesteads in this road no less than seventy men have replied to the call. At No 52 Mr

> and Mrs George and Ellen Hackett have five sons serving (Albert, Killed in Action, 1916) and one Corporal Hackett, had frozen feet in March 1915. Recovering he entered the trenches a second time, three days later he stopped one in the left shoulder and after a long and painful illness is back in the firing line again.'

Other families included Mrs Thorne, No 8, four of whose six sons were in the Royal Sussex Regiment, another in the Royal Marines, whilst Able Seaman S E Thorne served on HMS *Indomitable.*

Mrs Thorne also had eight brothers serving.

Mrs King, a widow of a Special Police Sergeant living in Essex Road, also had six sons serving: two were sailors, 'of whom Ernest, the last one, has just been recalled, he was one of the Bognor dustmen who had previously served as a sailor for fourteen years'. Of her four soldier sons, Private George King did not return (Killed in Action, 1915).

The Young family sent four sons, one of whom served with the Royal Field Artillery. Another was sent to Canada, working there in a munitions factory. Of the other two, one serving with the Royal Berkshire Regiment was invalided home having lost his right leg, right arm and the use of his left leg. The last son, Sergeant G Young DCM, fell on the battlefield (Date Unknown).

CHAPTER 10

Aftermath

Gradually, life in Bognor began to return to normal as the soldiers and sailors were demobbed from their various regiments and ships. Many men of the Royal Sussex Regiment returned during 1919, the 2nd Battalion in April, having been abroad since August 1914. Crowds of people and flag waving children turned out to greet them as they marched to the Chichester Cross to a great reception by the Mayor. They had been part of the original Expeditionary Force and had been

Peace Day celebrations.

abroad throughout the war. The 1st Battalion arrived at the end of the year, following six years in India and Mesopotamia and surviving a cholera epidemic shortly before returning. They and the other battalions, which were disbanded as the Regiment returned to a peacetime role, all received enthusiastic and emotional homecomings when they arrived at Chichester Railway Station and marched through the City back to their Barracks. The 7th Battalion arrived home on 18 June 1919 and an especially warm welcome was afforded the 4th Battalion on their return in August. Containing many local men, they had been kept in Germany 'in readiness to advance in the event of the Germans failing to accept the peace settlement'.

Suddenly Bognor was full of young men all eager to get on with their lives. Nationally, several ex-servicemen's organisations had been formed, two of which received good support in the town.

The Comrades of the Great War

The Comrades of the Great War, a non political organisation, was formed in 1917 'to represent the rights of the ex-serviceman'. Locally, an inaugural meeting was held at the Queens Hall; the movement 'was to band together all discharged soldiers and to carry on in their civilian life the comradeship they had learnt in the trenches and camps'.

Quickly attracting a large local membership, a social club at the Arcade Hall was planned:

> 'A very necessary club is to be founded at the Arcade Hall, under the distinguished patronage of Colonel H D Fryer, JP., the President, who is assisted in this good effort by practically all the prominent residents of this district. Excellent Headquarters have been selected, it being practically impossible to secure a more central situation or better accommodation as the premises is electrically illuminated and has every convenience, canteen space, room for recreation, reading, writing and a Common Room.'

Although the premises had been secured it still needed furnishing and several fund raising events took place, including a 'Grand Vaudeville Concert' held at the Kursaal. Membership to the club was extended to servicemen from earlier campaigns who were welcomed as 'Old Comrades'. The subscriptions were maintained 'at a very moderate level and should prove a good investment to those who are available for membership'. As well as being a social and recreative place, an employment bureau was established for the urgent task of helping Comrades to find work and 'interesting lectures and addresses' were held to further this aim. The club side was to 'keep alive the glorious spirit which has existed in all stations of life during the troublesome period of the Great War'.

The Club opened on the first Saturday of February 1919 with an informal music night, when forty discharged servicemen became members, the Secretary welcoming them and announcing the club would be open for their enjoyment and relaxation every night at 7pm. Within a couple of weeks the membership had reached one hundred and twenty. The Comrades also formed a football team, playing a Charity Match against the Railwaymen, to help raise funds for the War Memorial Hospital. The match took place at Wingate's Field, Victoria Drive, the comrades proving too strong, running out 7-0 winners, there was a 'fairly good attendance and a substantial sum was raised'. Their achievements on the football field attracted the attention of the *Portsmouth Football Mail*:

> 'Twenty-two discharged soldiers turned out at Emsworth on Saturday and provided the best football seen for several seasons.'

The National Federation of Discharged and Demobilized Sailors and Soldiers

The National Federation of Discharged and Demobilized Sailors and Soldiers formed a local branch in April 1917, meeting at the Belmont Restaurant. Known as brothers, they attracted nearly one hundred and sixty members and welfare was their main priority. They also opened a club in February 1919, offering memberships to all ex-servicemen, who could enjoy the facilities every evening from 6.00pm. Their opening night took the form of a smoking concert followed by a sing-along with Brother King on the piano.

These two new clubs spelt the end for the Welcome Club run by the Women's Institute in Waterloo Square, which had done so much to entertain and care for soldiers and sailors during the dark days. From June 1918 the Sunday Club was run by them alongside it and 8662 servicemen had visited by the time this closed in March 1919:

> 'A very pleasant evening was spent at the Bognor Welcome Club, when a large number of soldiers and sailors and discharged soldiers were entertained, the occasion being the last night of this very successful Club. The men were provided with a bounteous supply of cakes, sandwiches, sausage rolls, blancmanges and fruit salad. The ladies who had so kindly given their services to this institution and so ably contributed to its successful work will carry on their patriotic work at the new Old Comrades Club.'

Finding Employment

Apart from the social side of the two new organisations, the more serious problem of helping ex-servicemen returning home was not always easy. Finding employment was often difficult; one '1914 volunteer' complained bitterly in a letter to the *Bognor Observer*; he was one of several ex servicemen who had applied for a job, only to be told that the position was being kept open for 'another man' who was subsequently appointed:

> 'Is it possible that the English people are beginning to forget the men who gave their all to keep their homes still English, will the better England we were all led to believe we would come back to prove to be a mirage?'

There were cases of sharp practice amongst some local employers who, on finding that a number ex-servicemen were in receipt of a War Pension, offered them less money per week than they had paid a previous incumbent. Another source of friction concerned the large numbers of women working in shops 'doing work that disabled ex-servicemen could do'. Having stepped into the breach during the conflict to help keep Bognor's shops functioning, many women were reluctant to lose their incomes now that the men had returned. With so many ex-servicemen now unemployed, 'why were large numbers of women still employed in shop work?' was an often asked question. Under a Government scheme, war widows were given training to render them efficient in a remunerative occupation provided they were in receipt of a minimum pension, on top of which allowances were made towards their uniforms, equipment or books.

These and many cases like them were part of the welfare workload of the two ex-servicemen's organisations and were mirrored across the country, a workload which was embraced nationally in May 1921 when the British Legion was formed, both the Comrades and the Federation Clubs disbanding in favour of the Legion.

Housing

The housing of many soldiers returning to their families and settling down to married life did cause some problems. The Council were building new properties and twelve built on the site of Geals Brickyard became Mons Avenue, after the first battle of the war and applications were invited from ex-servicemen or widows to apply for tenancy, preference being given to those having children and 'at present living in apartments'. All those interested were to send in details of their current housing conditions, Army, Navy and Air Force service number and the ages of their children. The rent for the new houses was to be 14s 6d per week.

The Church Lads' Brigade

The Church Lads' Brigade received a special mention in the local press in January 1919. In the early stages of the war their band was a familiar sight leading the recruiting rallies around the town and many of their members went into the forces. Now they too were disbanding:

> 'Bognor has reason to be proud of the Church Lads' Brigade members in the past terrible years. Its members were amongst the first to come forward in the Country's hour of need with over one hundred and twenty serving the Colours. Four received Officers' commissions and many became NCOs. One obtained the Croix de Guerre and two others the Distinguished Conduct Medal. Seventeen made the great sacrifice and a fitting memorial is to be placed in the Parish Church. Major Panter OC.'

The Red Cross

The Bognor Red Cross stood down from its war footing and its work at Graylingwell ceased in March 1919. Throughout the conflict twelve ladies had performed daily duties there with Miss Mary Hay and Miss Grace Cutis being singled out for special praise, whilst Miss Burgess, the Lady Superintendent, received the Royal Red Cross Medal from the King:

> 'It is with great regret that Miss Hay has had to resign her position as Quartermaster of the Women's Red Cross Detachment. Miss Hay threw herself into the work of making the Detachment thoroughly efficient from the days when no one was expecting a war and it was difficult to persuade people of the importance of preparing for it. It speaks highly of her enthusiasm that when the Graylingwell War Hospital was opened the authorities were glad to call upon the Bognor Detachment to work there and they continued to do so throughout the war.'

As well as supplying many volunteers to work at the Graylingwell War Hospital, the Bognor Red Cross raised monies for ambulances and other war causes despite losing 'a good many members who had left to serve in the army'. One member, the architect Mr Tufnell, who had a business in the High Street, was turned down for military service on health grounds. Undaunted, he volunteered for service in France as a Red Cross ambulance driver. In January 1917 *The Bognor Observer* reported that he had been 'promoted to Officer Commanding the largest Red Cross convoy in France at the present time and on this fact he will receive the cordial congratulations of all the residents of Bognor'. At the end of the war he was made a Member of the British Empire for his work in France as a volunteer driver.

Two other members also volunteered: Mr Sinnott had been on munitions and had rendered first aid at a big accident at a munitions works and Mr H H Kent, of the Thatched Cottage, Aldwick Avenue, helped in a more personal way. A pioneer motorist, he voluntarily gave his services and his motor car to help the Red Cross, travelling to France at his own expense, to aid with the evacuation of injured soldiers.

The Volunteer Organisations Disband

The Bognor Volunteer Workers Association held their final meeting and published their impressive war record. Since 1914 they had produced 1183 mufflers, 432 pairs of socks, 327 sets of headgear, 270 pairs of mittens, 4 pairs of cutis, 6 pairs of operating stockings, 2 pairs of bed socks, 33 bed jackets, 544 pocket handkerchiefs, 526 hospital bags, 509 pairs of slippers, 314 anti vermin vests, 71 suits of pyjamas, 64 flannel shirts, 35 helpless case jackets, 18 dressing gowns, all handmade and supplied to Graylingwell War Hospital. In addition, some 20,000 other items were made and many books collected and sent to the Front, a remarkable achievement. At the winding up meeting they donated all their surplus funds to the two ex service clubs and the Bognor War Memorial fund.

The Hothampton War Hospital Supply Depot, which had been operating since 1916, also closed. It had specialised in making war dressings and had supplied over 13, 000 of them to the Horsham Depot; 'We have indeed been most grateful for all the valuable help you have given us and so have the various hospitals to which we have sent the beautiful things you have sent us.'

The Bognor Town Band

Having packed its instruments away in 1914 when the band members went to war, a movement was on foot to reform, 'as many of the old members are now back again in Bognor from the war'. The Bognor Council took an interest in its reformation, with the Clerk to the Council, Mr Jubb, taking a leading role. Soon a Band Committee was formed and £100 expended on instruments and music, with a new bandmaster appointed with a salary of £50 per annum. Within a few months the sound of the Bognor Town Band was again heard on Bognor seafront, playing its first concerts during Easter 1919, 'making a very succesful debut, playing to large audiences'.

Bognor Cricket Club

Having been closed down for the duration, a public meeting was called in the spring of 1919 at the Town Hall to attempt 'to re-establish the pastime of cricket in Bognor'. It had been a close thing during the war as to whether the ground would survive, having been utilised for agricultural work, but it was suggested that it could be made serviceable again 'by June'. That was the good news. The bad news followed, when the meeting was reminded that the Club was still in debt of £50 from before the war, had lost most of its equipment and at least a further £100 was needed to 'resuscitate' the Club, putting the ground in order and patching up the derelict pavilion so that it might last a year or two longer. The last time it had been used for match teas before the war the floor gave way!

However, the spirit to revive the Club prevailed, with fund raising commencing immediately and further meetings arranged to obtain fixtures. The sound of leather on willow was heard again in Bognor that summer.

Peace Celebrations

Saturday 19 July 1919, was the day the Government announced that national Peace Celebrations would take place. Over the previous six months various committees in Bognor were hard at work organising the day's events to make it 'a festive and happy occasion'.

The festivities began with the firing of twenty one maroons at 9am in Waterloo Square by the 'zealous members of the Bognor Fire Brigade'. By this time a little rain was falling, but that did not dampen the procession, which commenced at 11am 'on the dot' and was said to have been the largest ever staged in the town, led by the Band of 2nd Battalion the Scots Guards. It was as if the whole town was taking part, both in organisations military and civilian, with individual entries too numerous to mention. The procession stopped for a few minutes at the Eastern Bandstand on the Esplanade where a short service was conducted and after the National Anthem continued to the west end.

At 2pm the children assembled at their respective elementary schools where they were presented with commemorative medals, after which they were 'marched' to Wingate's Field in Victoria Drive, where an afternoon of children's sports took place, 'providing much amusement for the spectators as well as the children'.

Throughout most of the day the rain held off but became heavier, cutting short the children's sports, but did not spoil their tea of bread and butter and cake, provided by voluntary donations, with the Girl Guides doing the washing up!

In the evening an illuminated carnival procession took place in heavy rain, followed by more fireworks set off on the pier. The day ended with ten flares 'provided by the Government' which 'brilliantly illuminated' the town for nearly an hour whilst the record crowds made their way home. Despite the weather, it was a day which lingered long in the memory of many Bognorians.

The Peace Celebrations at North Bersted took place three weeks later, courtesy of Mr Sait of Rookery Farm, 'who gave the parishioners a grand treat'. The festivities commenced at 2pm with children's races, entertainment by the Bognor Clown, followed by adult races and tea.

> 'The farm hands were then marshalled in front of their employer, who spoke a few kindly, sensible words, interspersed with jokes to each and he then presented ten of his regular employees with a silver medal each and the others with monetary presents.'

Finally, three hundred quarter-pound tins of sweets were distributed amongst the children, each tin inscribed 'Rookery Farm, Bognor, Peace Celebrations, 7 August 1919'.

CHAPTER 11

The War Memorials

Throughout the war there had been discussions as to what form a War Memorial would take when the time came to erect one. With the war less than six months old and the casualty numbers beginning to rise, Bognor Council initiated a temporary Roll of Honour 'to be held in the Town Hall and inscribed from time to time with the names of soldiers, sailors and others who have given their lives for the service of their Country in this present war'. This was placed in the Council Chamber and when completed at the end of the war it was to be illuminated and then hung in a place of honour. The Council also had other plans.

In December 1916 the Bognor Council's Surveyor was instructed to contact a number of local firms who fitted shop fronts regarding the making of a War Memorial to contain a Roll of Honour of those who had lost their lives in the war, in accordance with a pre-approved design. Subsequently three tenders were submitted, ranging from £30 to £60, the cheapest being accepted. The temporary war shrine, which was erected outside the Council Offices, was nearly seven feet high and four feet wide and made of mahogany, with three divisions for names. In the centre was a Union Jack with the words 'For his Country's Sake' and the shrine was surmounted by bronze figures representing various branches of the service. Two years later the Council's thoughts turned to a more permanent Memorial.

The matter came before the Council in the spring of 1918, when the Surveyor presented a full-sized drawing of the proposed shrine, 'every detail was shown and was well thought out'. The Special Purposes Committee will meet at an early date to deal with the question of a site after which the work will be proceeded with. The shrine is classic in design and the Roll of Honour contains space for 500 names. the structure will be surmounted by a group of bronze statues representing the services, the Navy, Army, Colonial Forces and Nurses, under which will be the words 'For his Country's Sake' and the Union Jack'.

The Bognor War Memorial Hospital

Another scheme was also in people's minds. A cottage hospital was needed in the town and the idea of combining this with a War Memorial gathered pace. The week the war ended, Mr Frank Lemmon, a draper from High Street who had lost two sons in the war, wrote to the paper supporting the cottage hospital idea:

> 'Sir. Now the accomplishment of a satisfactory peace is so near to hand is it not time for the inhabitants of Bognor to consider what means they will take to perpetuate the memory of those who have so freely given their lives for us all?
>
> I make a suggestion which appeals to my wife, my family and myself and may, I hope, appeal to other residents of the town. It seems to be generally acknowledged that a cottage hospital is urgently required for the District. Why not make such a building our thanks offering for the restoration of peace and at the same time incorporate with it the War Shrine which has been so much discussed. To me it appears to be a quite appropriate way of showing gratitude to the memory of those who have given everything for us and be of incalculable benefit to the town and neighbourhood. An ordinary Memorial erection by itself would be, to many, a more or less useless expense. Incorporated with a building which may be used for the alleviation of suffering for all time would more thoroughly serve the purpose. I am prepared, on behalf of my wife and myself to donate a yearly substantial sum which I consider to be sound and practicable. Our offer is absolutely contingent upon the incorporation of the two schemes.
>
> Frank Lemmon.'

In the end, Bognor had both the hospital and a permanent War Memorial. The War Memorial Hospital came first 'in the honoured

Lemmon's drapers shop in High Street.

memory of the men of Bognor and District who in the Great War gave their lives for us and for the cause of liberty'.

Mr Fleming of Aldwick Grange, had promised £7000 if the town raised £2000. The project soon attracted fund raising events and 'donations flooded in from all quarters'. Frank Bale, the Bognor clown, whose son Arthur was killed on the Somme, became a leading mover.

Throughout 1918 the search was on for suitable premises, the Council eventually settling on a house, Springfield, at South Bersted on the Chichester Road, which was purchased and converted from a family home to a hospital with four wards, an operating theatre, staff rooms and offices. In July 1919 the War Memorial Hospital was opened. Over seven hundred people attended the opening ceremony, conducted by Mrs J Fleming, accompanied by the Band of 2nd Battalion the Royal Scots Fusiliers, who played in the grounds during the afternoon whilst the teas were being served.

On handing over the key to Mrs Fleming, the Reverend T Ross said:

> 'This key will let in the people of Bognor to the hospital, ill and sometimes despairing, but I hope they will come out of the door in health and hopeful.'

The War Memorial Hospital and staff.

On entering the hall by the front door the first thing to attract attention was the fine Memorial Tablet, on which was to be placed the names of those from Bognor and District who had fallen in the war. And here there was a problem; nobody knew at that time just how many names would eventually need to be listed, a problem compounded when the Council realized that, despite the roll of the fallen having been started early in the war, it had not been kept up to date. An appeal to correct this was made in *The Bognor Observer* with the help of the Red Cross:

> 'In connection with the tablet to the memory of Bognor men who have fallen in the Great War that is to be erected in the hospital, we find that the Parish Council has a list of one hundred and fifty names and the (Town) Council have all the names up to a certain date, but no absolute and reliable list exists. May we therefore through your columns ask that residents whose husbands, brothers or sons have fallen in the war to send the following particulars at once - their number, rank, Christian name and surname, (not initials), also the unit or ship and date of death. Names should be sent to the Quartermaster of the Women's Detachment of the Red Cross, Miss Hay, at Ravenswood, Neville Road, Bognor.'

The Memorial Tablet was subsequently completed, listing three hundred and twenty four names, which include some duplication of names that also appear on other local War Memorials.

The Bognor Town War Memorial

Oswald Bridges, the Council Surveyor, arranged for a temporary Cenotaph to be erected 'in the large space at the end of the High Street, opposite the Bedford Hotel in Waterloo Square', in readiness for the first anniversary of the Armistice in 1919. On it were placed two large laurel wreaths and the inscription, 'their names liveth for evermore'. Photographs were produced, copies of which were sold for one shilling, the proceeds donated towards the proposed War Memorial Hospital. The Cenotaph was removed soon afterwards, to be returned in 1920 when over two hundred wreaths were placed on it.

The temporary war memorial used for two years.

The Council then announced that they would provide a permanent site for a Cenotaph 'if the residents could find the money'. Mr Bridges again took the lead, declaring that he would draw up the plans at no cost and personally donate five guineas towards the project. An appeal was launched, the *Bognor Observer* urging each man, woman and child to give 'at least a penny' when collectors called at their houses on 13 December 1920. Forty-seven collectors toured the town, 'the day being one of the worst possible from the weather point of view'. The appeal was kept open for a few more weeks, closing with the magnificent total of £260 16s 7d.

The site promised by the Council had yet to be finalized. One option, the Steyne, was soon eliminated, leaving two more possibilities, both in Waterloo Square, which was also proposed to become a War Memorial pleasure ground. One option, at the southern end, was favoured by the Council, but not by the public or many ex-servicemen:

> 'It is lamentable to set it at the south end, so close to the Pier entrance, the most ribald position in town, where char-a-bancs pick up and set down their passengers. We want a spot where, if necessary, people could pray.'

The second site in Waterloo Square was then chosen, in the north east corner, the pleasure gardens idea being shelved and with Armistice Day 1921 approaching, work proceeded apace in preparing the ground. A meeting of the top subscribers was held in the Arcade Club in May 'to choose a design'. The Cenotaph itself was to be made of the finest Cornish silver granite.

The official unveiling ceremony took place on Armistice Day, half an hour before the two minutes' silence. The ex-Servicemen, wearing their medals 'by permission of His Majesty the King', fell in at the Bedford Street Drill Hall, where many had been recruited a few years earlier and marched to the Cenotaph.

Special arrangements were made for the war widows and their children, many of them wearing their husband's or father's medals, to occupy a prime position for the ceremony. They were joined by over a thousand school children who had walked there, accompanied by their school teachers, from all parts of Bognor. Tradesmen closed their shops from ten o'clock until midday as the whole town came to a standstill.

1914
1918
TO THE MEMORY OF THE
GLORIOVS DEAD
OF BOGNOR & DISTRICT

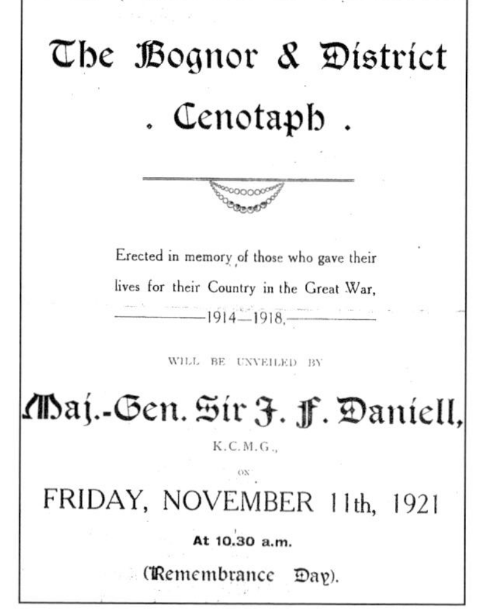
The Bognor & District
. Cenotaph .

Erected in memory of those who gave their
lives for their Country in the Great War,
1914—1918,

WILL BE UNVEILED BY

Maj.-Gen. Sir J. F. Daniell,
K.C.M.G.,

ON

FRIDAY, NOVEMBER 11th, 1921

At 10.30 a.m.

(Remembrance Day).

'Remembrance Day, the third anniversary of the Armistice, was solemnly observed all over the British Empire, but nowhere could the Honour to the Glorious Dead have been more sincerely accorded and with more smoothness of detailed ceremonial than at Bognor, on the occasion of the unveiling of a Cenotaph provided by public subscription. No further commendation of the able and thoughtful work of the organisers can be made than this statement. The whole ceremony was impressive and carried out without a hitch, evoking heartfelt tribute and grateful feelings of the population of Bognor in the memory of the fallen. A scene which must be imprinted on the appreciative minds of the many relatives of the Bognor dead, who took part in the poignant proceedings.'

On Friday morning foregathered a large concourse of the people of Bognor and District, representative of all classes and creeds. It was a bitterly cold day, with bright sunshine. The whole precincts of Waterloo Square were thronged, with accommodation reserved for the schoolchildren of Bognor, Bersted, Felpham and Pagham. A procession started from the Arcade, comprising the Boy Scouts and Bugle Band, the Girl Guides, Yeomanry Signallers and Territorials, the Bognor Town Band, on one of its first parades since reforming, Red Cross workers and a large number of ex-Servicemen wearing their medals. On one side of the Cenotaph, room was found for the relatives of the Fallen, some of whom wore the medals of their loved ones. On either side of the Cenotaph stood the Coastguards men with the Town Officials, and promptly at 10.30 the proceedings began with the Bognor Town Band's impressive rendering of Chopin's *Marche Funbre*. The dedication and prayers were lead by the Vicar of South Bersted. The unveiling of the Cenotaph was performed by Major-General Sir J F Daniell KCMG, the son of a previous vicar of Aldingbourne, who in his address said:

'You have come here today to commemorate the gallant men, over three hundred, who went from this town and district to do their duty in the cause of Justice, Right and Freedom, who did that duty nobly and well and gave all they could, even their lives. Their places at home can be filled no more, but they have left to those who loved them and they have left to the Country they died to save a proud and I trust undying memory.

'You in Bognor have in your War Memorial Scheme done two great things. You have your War Memorial Hospital, which will be I know an untold blessing to the sick and suffering and today you unveil your Cenotaph, an act of pure commemoration of the dead.'

'It was now close to eleven o'clock and there was a momentary wait until the maroon signalled the two minutes' silence. The hymn 'For All the Saints, Who From Their Labours Rest' was then sung, led by the Town Band. After a short address and prayers there came the singing of the familiar and inspiring hymn 'O God Our Help in Ages Past'. The sad relatives then stepped forward to find the names of their loved ones on the Cenotaph, as the rest of those present quietly departed.'

The whole event was 'excellently filmed' and shown at the Picturedrome for the rest of the week.

Felpham War Memorial

Meanwhile, the individual parishes were also planning their own tributes; after all, this war had touched every street, place of employment and almost every family.

Proposals for honouring the thirty-nine heroes from Felpham and Middleton initially centred around a Memorial Village Hall, land for which in Limmer Lane was offered by Robert Sadler, the owner of Church Farm. However, this scheme was considered to be too expensive at the time and after much discussion the decision was made, provided the necessary funding could be raised, to build one or possibly two War Memorial Cottages, occupancy preference to be given to 'the men who have fought in the war and their dependants, who through poverty or misfortune should be in need of such assistance. The cottages will be a record of their appreciation to those of their fellow

James Hale, a Trustee of the War Memorial Cottages.

countrymen who resided in the Parish and who fell in the service of their Country.'

Once again a suitable piece of land was offered by Robert Sadler, this time on the east side of Flansham Lane. The fund set up to meet the building costs soon attracted contributions, eventually realising £694 10s 1d; the cottages cost £517 17s to build, architects and other fees being waived. Twelve trustees were appointed to 'allocate and look after the residents' and to invest the balance of monies into an endowment fund for the general upkeep of the cottages and the laying out of the gardens with fruit trees. Among the trustees was James Hale, a local carrier, coal merchant, Parish Councillor, school manager and a leading light in the local nonconformist chapel. Others included a retired dance teacher, a retired butler and the local butcher, Mr Ruff.

Building took place with a certain amount of help from Mr Richardson, the landlord of the Fox Inn, Felpham, who was also a skilled bricklayer. Another helper was the local plumber, Henry Witcher, who lived close by in Flansham Lane. The first resident, Mrs Ashcroft, took possession in 1922 for an annual rent of one shilling.

A Memorial in the form of a large brass plate is also in St Mary's Church, Felpham and contains the names of the fallen.

North Bersted War Memorial

A meeting was held in June 1919 to ascertain what form a war memorial for North Bersted should take. One popular idea was a recreation ground 'for the lads', but as a football and cricket pitch already existed, this idea was eventually shelved. It was then proposed to erect a War Memorial. A further meeting was held in October when it was announced that subscriptions amounting to £84 12s had been raised and consent was being sought to erect a Memorial in the church grounds. By November consent had not been obtained, which caused a degree of annoyance and in an adjourned meeting a week or so later it was decided to place a tablet in memory of the fallen inside the church.

The unveiling took place on Sunday, 17 October 1920, at the evening service, led by the Reverend FTP Evershed:

> 'There was an overflow congregation, a special form of service was arranged and the ceremony took place in the middle of it. The tablet is of Repousse brass, which means that the whole of the ornaments and letters are raised and is the most valuable and artistic form of tablet used for ecclesiastical work. The tablet is mounted on a dove marble back, shaped to the design of the tablet and fixed to the right hand side of the entrance. It was executed and fixed by Mr A Seymour, a monumental mason, of Bognor. The tablet was covered by a Union Jack and surrounded by a number of large and lovely wreaths. The ceremony was performed by Mrs Winter, who for many years has resided in North Bersted and is one of the oldest inhabitants. The Last Post was sounded by Mr R Pollington and at the close of the service the Dead March in Saul was played by Mr Cross on the organ, with Mr R I Sharpe, violin and Mr R C Sharpe, cello.'

South Bersted War Memorial

South Bersted Church also had a brass memorial tablet bearing the names of all those from the Parish who had made the supreme sacrifice.

> 'On Sunday afternoon, Advent Sunday (1919), South Bersted Church was crowded on the occasion of a special service of unveiling and dedication of a War Memorial Tablet to perpetuate

the memory of the fallen heroes of the Parish. The large and handsomely engraved tablet, designed by Mr W Tillot Barlow, is of brass mounted on oak and through the loving labours of Messrs C Hemingfield and W White has been attached to the wall just inside the north door. It commemorates the great sacrifice of no less than one hundred and four men of South Bersted, twenty-five of whom were married, while over six hundred had joined up before conscription was enforced. The tablet, which on Sunday was surrounded by floral tributes, bears the following inscription:

"In honoured memory of the men of South Bersted Parish
who gave their lives for their King and Country
in the Great War, 1914 to 1918"

'The Vicar, the Reverend FTP Evershed, accompanied from the choir by Mr RO White, who had lost a son in the war and was wearing his medal, proceeded to the north entrance where Mrs Powell, of Rose Cottage, Ivy Lane, who had lost three sons in the war, unveiled the Tablet'.

The Parish also raised money to build the South Bersted Memorial Hall, which was opened on 26 October 1921 when 250 persons sat down for a supper, followed by a concert.

Pagham War Memorial

Finally at Pagham, where a memorial to the twenty men who lost their lives, in the form of a Celtic stone cross with a Sword of Sacrifice on its front face, placed on a base and plinth, was erected in the grounds of the St Thomas A'Becket Church. The Memorial contains the full names of all those who died on the front and was unveiled and dedicated on Sunday 20 February 1921 in the presence of the Dean of Chichester, who was the preacher. The unveiling was performed by Mrs Whiffen of Barn Rocks. Inside the Church are listed the names of all the men from Pagham who served in the Great War.

The Pagham War Memorial.

Index